**Also available from Mark Allard
Regressions**

LIVING MYTHOS
THE ART OF SELF-REALIZATION

MARK ALLARD

BALBOA
PRESS
A DIVISION OF HAY HOUSE

Copyright © 2017 Mark Allard.

All rights reserved. No part of this book may be used or reproduced by any means, graphic, electronic, or mechanical, including photocopying, recording, taping or by any information storage retrieval system without the written permission of the author except in the case of brief quotations embodied in critical articles and reviews.

Image Credit: Jenn Borton

Balboa Press books may be ordered through booksellers or by contacting:

Balboa Press
A Division of Hay House
1663 Liberty Drive
Bloomington, IN 47403
www.balboapress.com
1 (877) 407-4847

Because of the dynamic nature of the Internet, any web addresses or links contained in this book may have changed since publication and may no longer be valid. The views expressed in this work are solely those of the author and do not necessarily reflect the views of the publisher, and the publisher hereby disclaims any responsibility for them.

The author of this book does not dispense medical advice or prescribe the use of any technique as a form of treatment for physical, emotional, or medical problems without the advice of a physician, either directly or indirectly. The intent of the author is only to offer information of a general nature to help you in your quest for emotional and spiritual well-being. In the event you use any of the information in this book for yourself, which is your constitutional right, the author and the publisher assume no responsibility for your actions.

Any people depicted in stock imagery provided by Thinkstock are models,
and such images are being used for illustrative purposes only.
Certain stock imagery © Thinkstock.

Print information available on the last page.

ISBN: 978-1-5043-9133-7 (sc)
ISBN: 978-1-5043-9134-4 (e)

Balboa Press rev. date: 12/13/2017

Dedicated to:

Robert Harry Fernand Viau

November 11, 1962 - August 1, 2006

For showing me a path through the trees.

"Welcome to Immortality"

Table of Contents

Foreword xi
Acknowledgements xv
Prologue xvii

örlög ~ fate 1
tvískiptur ~ duality 19
þýðir ~ meaning 66
Ragnarök 149

Epilogue 169
Footnotes 183
Bibliography 191
Appendix A 199
Regressions 205

"The world hangs by a thin thread, and that thread is the psyche of man... nowadays, we are not threatened by elemental catastrophes... we are the great danger. The psyche is the great danger. What if something goes wrong with the psyche? And so, it is demonstrated in our day what the power of the psyche is, how important it is to know something about it. But we know nothing."

~ C.G. Jung

"At some point in my degree, it occurred to me that I was learning the standardized Western/classical perspective of history and—to some extent—I think the omission of major ancient mythologies from the traditional sphere of scholarly discourse now gives them an air of the occult. Specifically, it gives the impression that Celtic and Norse religions were somehow more 'pagan' in comparison to their Greek and Roman counterparts."

~ Tallia Chau

"I find it so tragic and ironical that the age in which we live should regard the word 'myth' and 'illusion' as synonymous, in view of the fact that the myth is the real history... The myth is the tremendous activity that goes on in humanity all the time, without which no society has hope or direction, and no personal life has a meaning."

~ Laurens van der Post

"If I've been at all responsible for people finding more characters in themselves that they originally thought they had, then I'm pleased, because that's something I feel very strongly about. That one isn't totally what one has been conditioned to think one is. That there are many facets of the personality that many of us have trouble finding."

~ David Bowie

Foreword

If you've ever wondered "Is it possible to innovate my own mind?" you're exploring the right resource. What lies within these pages is an autobiographical and lucid thesis on how to do just that: to create a mind of your own choosing.

There are non-fiction books that combine theories to offer a new approach. There are non-fiction records of people who've lived their accounts and reported back to us their key learnings. And then there are publications that do both. Living Mythos *is one of these.*

This book is about removing the psychological, historical beliefs and mythological boundaries to make meaningful progress in our lives. It's an approach that puts us in the driver's seat to have the impact and be the contribution to others that we desire.

I've witnessed Mark apply his intimate understanding of the contents of these pages to transform and re-create his own life over the past four years. I believe what he puts forward can and will change you if you go into it with that intention. And like all meaningful innovation, only two things matter: execution and results. This man is a true creator who has made an art out of the one thing many artists struggle with: taking the vision into the world so that it can be experienced by others.

From Jung to myth, ego to values, Mark delivers an understanding of how all of these elements (and many others) influence—or more accurately, dictate—our behaviours. We come to a better understanding of ourselves, others, and how we might just use our own free will to influence those around us for the better as we move forward on our respective adventures.

I wish us all fulfilling adventures!

~ Les Mottosky

Editors Preface

Mark has delivered profound insight through the ideologies of Norse mythology, his own personal adventures, and delicious, thought-provoking conversation. Our attention is turned inward, to the intimate space of our unique internal dialogues, where we are encouraged to use the tools he's offered to regain control of our ever-wandering focus, getting us back to our authentic Self.

Wonderfully thoughtful, Living Mythos *challenges us to achieve and maintain our ideal state.*

Mark, thank you with my whole heart for creating such an enjoyable, entertaining read that has enhanced my life lessons exponentially, right when I needed the guidance.

I am honoured to have had the opportunity to work with you on this incredible journey.

The experience and our friendship are precious to me . . .

~ Tara Albrecht

Acknowledgements

Tara Albrecht,* a brilliant editor, for continuously supporting my creative projects and ensuring my thoughts are accessible to others.

Olivier Balmokune, for encouragement and instigating change.

Jeff Brey, for the illustration in the dedication.

Jennifer Borton,* for creating marvelous symbols and diagrams from my doodles.

Yvonne Chapman, for being available at the right time and caring enough.

Tallia Chau,* for watering the seiðs.

Dad, for your courage to forsake all expectations of your upbringing in pursuit of personal value and meaning.

Graham Dunlop, for making your resources available.

Bruce Hatch, for answering endless questions and providing countless tools.

Trish Klein, for an opportunity bigger than myself.

Rye Lishewski,* for adventures.

Zeljko Matijevic, for a Jungian perspective.

Mom, for a lifetime of unconditional love, support, and introspection.

Les Mottosky,* for accountability.

Lon Parker,** for the introduction to Dada and your ongoing interest in expressions of absurdity as commentaries for what the majority call normal.

Ben Pearson,* for perspective and willingness.

Hallfríður J. Ragnheiðardóttir, for inspiration and memorable birthdays in Reykjavik.

Aaron Thibeault,** for always answering honestly.

Dr. Michael Yoon & **Dr. Jacquelyn Perron**, for helping synchronize my body with my mind.

To the cast* and crew** of *HNEFATAFL*, who brought to life the essence of *Living Mythos* through the medium of film, including **Philip Bowen, Jason Clark, Russell Chirckoff** and **Hussein Juma.**

Prologue

By the time our ancestors transitioned from hunter-gatherers into the agricultural revolution, ego had emerged from the unconscious—along with a set of archetypal images—of which human experience is woven. These archetypes are the foundation of mythology.

Move forward in time until you can begin to imagine yourself as a child, living in a small village in central Norway. For as long as you can remember, you've been told stories of the gods. These are more than just stories, though; they give meaning to hardship and value to celebration.

One day, there is great excitement in your village. News has come from a traveller that the goddess Freyja has been seen in these parts. She is probably searching for her wandering husband, you think to yourself.

A few days later, Freyja arrives. Others have come from neighbouring villages to be in the presence of the goddess. They bring gifts––offerings of friendship—with hopes that Freyja would bless them with fertility and prosperity.

You watch Freyja with fascination, following her every move. You even follow her when she moves to relieve herself, and are surprised that the gods must also go to the bathroom. From your hiding spot, you are puzzled to discover that Freyja has a penis. You do not mention a word of this to anyone, because you never should have been spying on the goddess.

What you don't know is that this is not really the goddess Freyja. This is a man from Sweden dressed up as a woman, cashing in on the vulnerability of those who are struggling to maintain value and meaning in a world that seems violently opposed to their existence.

Mythology is the story of consciousness evolving. Stories preserve the journey of consciousness from concept, to symbol, to manifested ideal.

The first forms of written language were symbols. For thousands of years, knowledge was passed from one generation to the next through symbols, which inspired story.

The letters we use today to form new *symbols of meaning* are relatively young in the history of our species, which is why the symbols of our ancestors remain so powerful.

In the essay, "Wotan,"[001] C.G. Jung wrote;

"Archetypes are like riverbeds which dry up when the water deserts them, but which it can find again at any time. An archetype is like an old watercourse along which the water of life has flowed for centuries, digging a deep channel for itself. The longer it has flowed in this channel, the more likely it is that sooner of later the water will return to its old bed."

This work has been inspired by a personal journey into psyche, as guided by mythology. I make no attempt to convince anyone of absolute truth. On the contrary, I believe "absolute truth" is, perhaps, the most perilous conception humans ever thought up. Absolutes continue to give rise to the cruelest of behaviours.

Throughout my research, I constantly discover references to the lack of centralized methodology or dogma among our ancient Northern ancestors. This allows for a fluid interpretation that is subjective in nature.

While religion attempts to confine intuition into a glass jar of absolutes and legalism, the richness of mythology is universal appeal to the individual; an offer to compare and contrast personal *experiences* with the internal archetypes of whichever pantheon of gods and goddesses resonates most.

"Stories are the way we, as humans, construct meaning. They're the way we make sense of our world."

~ Dr. Suzannah Lipscomb

"The study of mythology need no longer be looked upon as an escape from reality into the fantasies of primitive roles, but as a search for the deeper understanding of the human mind. In reaching out to explore the distant hills where the gods dwell and the depths where the monsters are lurking, we are discovering the way home." [012]

~ H.R. Ellis Davidson

ÖRLÖG

I

I

FATE

"In life, a man commits himself, draws his own portrait, and there is nothing but that portrait. No doubt this thought may seem comfortless to one who has not made a success of his life. On the other hand, it puts everyone in a position to understand that reality alone is reliable."

~ Jean-Paul Sartre

"Any journey toward lasting well-being and genuine contentment necessitates a deeper understanding of ourselves and others. Unless we start to understand what we profoundly need and why we need it, the journey cannot begin."

~ Dr. Bruno A. Cayoun

"Where does the truth of a person lie? Does it lie anywhere? As Sartre argues, we constantly invent, interpret, and reinterpret ourselves as we live. We also constantly invent, interpret, and reinterpret others by thinking, talking, and writing about them, both while they are alive and after they die. Perhaps that is all any of us are—an ongoing exercise in invention and interpretation undertaken by ourselves and others, until such time as we are dead and forgotten. People are impossible to pin down, which is what makes them so fascinating."

~ Gary Cox

Imagine you and a companion are seated in a theatre. This is opening night and there is not a spare seat in the house. Behind you, a couple has brought their two children. Both children are under seven; old enough to be constantly fidgeting in their seats and talking. They race up and down the aisles, as though the theatre were a grand playground.

You find yourself struggling to concentrate on the film. Do you turn around and say something to the parents? After all, everyone has paid money for admission and you are, likely, not the only one who has found his or her evening hijacked by this unanticipated disruption. Should you take the incentive? Wait for someone else? Does it even matter? Life is full of unanticipated disruptions. If you can't handle this, how will you handle the *real* problems?

We will return to this movie theatre a bit later.

My first book was released in October 2012. *Regressions* is the story of one man's journey through multiple versions of his life. He is unable to control this journey and begins to compare and contrast qualities of these distinct narratives in hopes of learning enough to make this transference stop, so he can find harmony with his love and peace with himself.

I think of *Regressions* as a modern fairy tale, and it may be understood as a metaphor for the Jungian concept of Individuation.

Individuation is ***"a process of transformation whereby the personal and collective unconscious are brought into consciousness, to be assimilated into the whole personality. It is a completely natural process necessary for the integration of the psyche."*** [#002]

Becoming the Character

Six months after *Regressions* was released, I began keeping track of patterns in my life. This began because I wanted to know if recognizable people appeared in my dreams at regular intervals. Soon, I was looking for patterns with the dedication of a mad scientist or a sane obsessive-compulsive. I kept track of impulses and cravings for everything from food and drugs, to sex and reading.

Over the next three-and-a-half years, no action or experience was immune from this microscope of my examination, and I began to notice cycles of behaviour that repeated on a daily, weekly, monthly, and even yearly basis.

Above all, this was an exercise in cultivating Self-awareness. I was motivated by an increased recognition of my habitual behaviour. This allowed me the choice to discard habits that were unsupportive of my **ideal state**.

Time, patience, and a willingness to avoid absolute convictions taught me that all tools can be weapons, and all weapons can be tools. True Self-empowerment is being able to recognize the impulses behind what drives our decisions and adjusting ourselves to maintain the necessary equilibrium for harmony—like tuning an instrument.

Your Inner Pantheon

"Freud viewed the unconscious as a place that was basically populated by fragmented personalities, not cognitive schemes of one form or another, and not processes, but things that were like living beings. You're alive, so you are composed of living subcomponents; they're fragmentary subpersonalities and each of them has their own worldview and rationalizations and emotional structure and goals and so that is why—when you get hungry—you see the world through the eyes of a hungry person and you think thoughts about food and your emotional reactions depend on whether food is available and whether it isn't and, maybe, whether or not the food you want is available, and that's nature imposing its necessities on you as a living being.

From a Jungian perspective, a lot of the forces that ancient peoples considered deities were personified representations of instinctual systems." [#003]

~ Jordan B. Peterson

Imagine your personality as an entire pantheon of gods. Each *quality of behaviour* competes for your attention. **Individuation** is a conscious understanding of these unconscious dialogues/impulses. Awareness brings the unconscious into consciousness, prompting the transcendence that religious systems allude to.

Good and evil are subjective distinctions based entirely on who is giving meaning to the words. What Stalin may have considered good might be in contrast to your own moral conclusion.

Consider the following descriptions and try not to associate them with anyone specifically: independence, freedom, knowledge, clever, light.

Now, consider these words without thinking of anyone specific: rebellious, deceptive, manipulation, destruction, war.

You have read two distinct descriptions associated with the same person, or rather, the same god. Can you guess which one? I'll give you a hint: this popular god is also described as a lion. (See [#004] for the answer.)

The point of this exercise is to remind us that most of what we embrace as truth is subjective. Absolutes are based on personal bias and experience. If our experiences differ—even if we are raised in the same home, city, and country—how much more extreme will our experience be when raised with different worldviews?

Your inner pantheon is as diverse as a political summit. Bureaucracy and judgement are intimate with one another, so any real progress can only happen when we dismiss these lovers.

You cannot harmonize your psyche if your rational brain is judging instinctual behaviours. Understanding is required. Understanding flows from, and creates, Self-awareness. Awareness of instinctual and/or habitual behaviour empowers us with the option of choice.

"As humans evolved, our brains didn't so much change as they grew. Evolution prefers to add on to what's created, rather than start from scratch. So, as humans required new skills, our primitive brain was not replaced with some completely new mode—the system of Self-control was slapped on top of the old system of urges and instincts. That means that for any instinct that once served us well, evolution has kept around, even if it now gets us into trouble." [#005]

~ Kelly McGonigal

Organized Misinformation

All dogma is propaganda. The structure offered by dogma is beneficial only if it produces discipline. The great majority pick and choose their theology, which renders dogma, at best, futile, and, at worst, a crutch.

Personal responsibility may be compromised when the events of life are given meaning from within the context of theology because dogma places a ceiling on awareness. It demands a resignation of personal power to a source outside Self, in spite of *being* a personification of forces within. As a result, we avoid accountability for our actions and the outcomes they produce. Without the weight of consequence, we disable the value of meaning.

"Freud recognized that the impulses we avoid or ignore would fight the hardest to be recognized, often manifesting in unnecessarily destructive ways. He described this unconscious process of manifesting as projecting. Carl Jung took this further by encouraging confrontation of the shadow side of our impulses.

Each of our archetypes has a shadow. Only by acknowledging all aspects of our personality can we fully integrate these impulses. Our awareness allows us to avoid being manipulated by these personalities." [#003]

~ Jordan B. Peterson

Each archetype has a shadow, expressing the **dual**-istic nature (polarity) of being.

Consciousness is a spectrum. Self-awareness facilitates participation in the unfolding conditions of our life.

The Observer Gets to Decide

"Observation of the experiment forces nature to collapse to one option or the other." [#006]

Let's return to the movie theatre, only this time, you are seated nine rows behind the couple with the two children. Perhaps you are *sympathizing* with the patrons seated closer, although you are far enough away that your experience has not been disrupted—unless *you choose* to pay attention to the drama unfolding at the front of the theatre. Suddenly, the man directly in front of the two children turns around and says something to their father. You can hear both men raise their voices and now they are on their feet.

We will return to this movie theatre a bit later.

The practice of becoming an observer—to detach from our experience or memory of an event—is woven through multiple spiritual and psychological disciplines. Why? Because we gain perspective by observing events, which, otherwise, would have gone unnoticed.

Imagine you were in a car accident. As the driver of the vehicle, your perspective and memory of the event will be quite different than the passenger, or someone across the street in a cafe, or the window washer fifty feet above the street who watched the whole event as he ate lunch.

Our perspective grows sharper by observing the perspective of others in contrast with our own. You cannot do this while trying to force your perspective on others or judging them for having their own. We may apply this same principle to our interactions with psyche. Without the perspective of each of our subpersonalities, we alienate information that has the potential to enrich our lives. A narrow point of view is like putting Self-awareness in a glass jar.

Building on Freud's understanding of subpersonalities, Carl Jung identified a series of archetypes associated with universal human impulses. These *qualities of behaviour* inspire the creation of **belief systems** as our conscious mind attempts to extract value and meaning from within these templates of experience.

Ego is threatened whenever belief systems are challenged. Belief systems may contradict each other. For example, religious and political beliefs often contradict personal beliefs. Emotional reactions to this conflict may form a **complex**, which is, essentially, a collection of thoughts that contain *qualities of behaviour*, which, together, create predictable scenarios.

We may disempower our complexes through the cultivation of Self-awareness. Jung called this process Individuation.

"*Complexes are part and parcel of who we are. The most we can do is become aware of how we are influenced by them and how they interfere with our conscious intentions. As long as we are unconscious of our complexes, we are prone to being overwhelmed or driven by them. When we understand them, they lose their power to affect us. They do not disappear, but over time their grip on us can loosen.*"

~ Daryl Sharp

The owner's manual for happily being human becomes tangible in the form of a map of our personality. In Greek mythology, Psyche is the goddess of the soul and is married to Eros, the god of love. This reaffirms the intimate relationship between Self-love and our inner pantheon.

The nature of our thoughts will always betray the belief systems at the root of our complexes. We may override all default or programmed belief systems by *intentionally* creating thought streams to replace unhealthy dialogues. In this way, we transform our destiny.

Recognition of the impulses (archetypes) that control our emotional reactions (complexes) is the first step towards building a map of our inner pantheon.

The Map is Not the Territory

General semantics "*provides a systematic methodology to understand how you relate to the world around you, how you react to this world, how you react to your reactions, and how you may adjust your behaviour accordingly.*

Your understanding of the world around you and how you choose to respond to the world is based on individual maps ... this map ... governs what you think, say, and do. The map can only be a partial representation of the actual possible territory, which is vast. In other words, one person's map can never fully express what is. The map can only express information filtered through an individual's perception." [007]

Whether you intentionally participated in its creation or not, your map is the means by which you may navigate the timestreams of being. To navigate, you must become aware of this map and intentionally use it to *navigate* through these templates of experience. Discipline cultivates mindfulness/Self-awareness, and supports willpower.

"Willpower has gone from being the thing that distinguishes us humans from animals, to the thing that distinguishes us from each other. People who have better control of their attention, emotions, and actions are better off almost any way you look at it." [005]

~ Kelly McGonigal

The choices we make are determined by the choices we have made, which, in turn, determine the choices we continue to make.

Subconscious behaviour is learned behaviour, and the subconscious makes no value judgement on the health or toxicity of decisions. Thus, becoming aware of our motivations and impulses is a necessary step towards making the unconscious, conscious.

"Conscious mind is reasoning will. Subconscious mind is instinctive desire–the result of past reasoning will." [008]

~ Charles Haanel

To be fair, you *can* go through life on autopilot. We are *all free* to settle into belief systems and, as long as we live within the boundaries of these systems, we will have a measure of contentment.

We are attracted to belief systems because they organize phenomena into a digestible system of solutions/answers to the most fundamental questions we have, such as: *Why am I here? What is my purpose?*

Belief system/illusion develops when we are unable to construct a "significance bridge" across the great chasm that exists between *experience* and the *value and meaning* required to rationalize experience. Alternately, existentialists [009] prefer to construct a unique bridge that is relevant and supportive of the ideal state they wish to create. This initiative demands emancipation from all forms of "absolute truth."

Absolute truth is the pacifier of the ignorant. Ignorance allows us to avoid personal responsibility, and makes it easy to justify blaming others for the conditions we encounter in life. Absolute truth is supported by illusion and threatened by knowledge.

"Words . . . define our reality; they define our worlds. We organize our lives and our words by concepts, by our thoughts about them, and we . . . think in terms of words. In this sense, at least, words make our reality and make our universe real." #010

~ Robert Moore and Douglas Gillette

A mathematician named Alfred Korzybski coined the term, *"the map is not the territory."* Maps are constructed by meaning, and we express meaning through words. Words are assigned meaning by individual experience, which makes them subjective, and conjures unique emotional reactions or responses. This is why the unconscious tends to speak to us *by means of dreams, active imagination, or free association, to be assimilated into the whole personality.*

The **territory** is the unlimited potential available to you as a result of free will. The collection of words that create our map may be understood as a sequence of belief systems that describe the motivation behind decisions.

"If you knew the definition of individual words but you didn't know how to turn those words into sentences and to turn those sentences into paragraphs, you would not have a meaningful story. If you don't know how the events of your life connect to a greater purpose and serve a greater context, then there is no sense to the story of your life."

~ David Aaron

"The map is not the territory" is a term which reminds us that we are not confined to the bias and prejudice of programmed belief systems (meaning

expressed through words) because the territory is as flexible and limitless as our willpower is strong.

Thinking is the beginning of Self-awareness. Self-awareness allows us to revise and update the map of our internal pantheon, which is necessary because experience constantly modifies the *significance* of the words we use to describe how we *feel*.

Impulse Control

You've left the theatre prematurely, and can admit things got out of hand. Having concentrated your attention on objects of frustration, frustration got the best of you.

While attempting to walk off your nerves, your companion suggests you try an exercise.

"Imagine your excitement, if you were one of those children. What a perfect evening this has been. Earlier, your family went to a restaurant and let you order anything you wanted. This is your younger sibling's birthday and you are delighted that you have the responsibility of supervising them.

Up on the big screen are incredible images of flying ships that have come to earth from outer space. You've just taken a drink from a large beverage and replaced it in the coaster when a man seated ahead of you turns around in his seat and says something to your dad. He sounds upset. Who could be upset in a movie theatre? Your dad says something and both men stand to their feet. They are shouting now, and suddenly the man swings out his arm and punches your dad across the face."

Since the publication of *Regressions*, my life has changed dramatically. Specifically, these changes have been a result of an emerging awareness; a by-product of tracking individual patterns.

Lest you assume this was easy, let me assure you that a lot of work was involved, and a lot of sacrifice. This is also the point. Discipline, work, and sacrifice, all foster awareness. This is how we begin to *build a bridge of meaning* for ourselves between our existence (being) and authenticity (meaning).

Awareness is cultivated through the practice of mindfulness, which anchors us in the present moment, preventing us from getting lost in the timestreams of our internal dialogues. **Internal dialogues** are responsible for creating the assumptions by which we limit others and ourselves.

Internal dialogues are supported by belief systems we have acquired, and the constant stream of thoughts that emerge from them. Our thoughts reflect what we pay attention to. What, and whom, we pay attention to can be said to possess us.

Observing tendencies *without judgement* allows us to notice patterns. Judgement is like introducing an uncontrolled factor into a controlled experiment—all measurable results will become distorted. Judgement is how we constantly sabotage our opportunity to break free of destructive cycles.

"Cycles don't mean free will is lost . . . the cycle is just a context, like a sunny day or a rainy day is the context for how we will live our day."

~ Walter Cruttenden

As soon as I tell you not to think of a red wagon, you already have. This is because thought moves faster than the speed of light. [011] While thought may arise from the unconscious, the choice to *entertain* thought is a conscious process.

Our thoughts are the cause, and conditions we experience in life are the effect. If you want to control the effect, you must control the cause. This demands a willingness to recognize and let go of toxic influences.

Replacing unsupportive inner dialogues with supportive ones is a matter of redirecting our attention from toxic influences towards those that support our ideal state.

A practical method to accomplish this is to remain teachable. Information we consume will eventually be recycled as thoughts, so absorb information that supports your ideal state, regardless of whether you logically understand it.

Synchronizing the triune brain is like getting the members of a team to agree on the same strategy. Willpower is the ability to control our impulses. This makes us more conscious of our experience. Who we are reflects our strategies for Self-control.

"Harmony in the world within means the ability to control our thoughts and to determine, for ourselves, how any experience may affect us. By taking mental possession, we come into actual possession." [#008]

~ Charles Haanel

Secret of the Norns

Patterns are best understood from the context of a specific time-oriented mindset—past, present, or future.

In Norse mythology, at one of the roots of the great tree, **Yggdrasil**, Three Norns carve out the destinies of all living beings in Runic symbols. Unlike their Greek counterparts—the Three Fates—destiny carved by the Norns is fluid, and can be transformed by the conduct and virtues of man. The dichotomy between these two worldviews is staggering.

"Three roots supported the great trunk, and one passed into the realm of the Æsir, a second into that of the frost giants, and a third into the realm of the dead. Beneath the root in giant-land was the spring of Mímir, whose waters contained wisdom and understanding. Óðinn has given one of his eyes for the right to drink a single draught of that precious water." [#012]

~ H.R. Ellis Davidson

Personal responsibility is a reflection of our understanding of free will. We may consider ourselves free even while maintaining a worldview that, fundamentally, restricts our freedom to a contained version of potential. This contained version of potential was one of Pandora's gifts to humanity. We refer to this gift as hope. It's easy to dismiss the consequences of behaviour when you have outsourced your fate to a belief system (or lack of one).

Our concepts of time—past, present, and future—are associated with distinct *qualities of behaviour.*

The Three Norns are named in regards to these respective time tenses. They are: *Urðr,* "What Once Was;" *Verðandi,* "What Is Coming Into Being;" and *Skuld,* "What Shall Be." [013]

Our tendency to behave in coordinated patterns (complexes) is a result of a specific, time-oriented mindset dominant in our life. The context from which to understand the effect is in understanding the cause. Behaviour is an effect not a cause. Behaviour may be healthy and supportive of our ideal happiness, or toxic. Healthy decisions are made when our triune mindsets/perspectives are in harmony.

The Overman

Personality forms as a result of the interaction between four functions that operate within psyche. One of these functions is referred to as the **Inferior Function**, because it is the part of our personality that is most intimate with the unconscious.

"One often finds the classic problem of the three and the four, about which Jung has written so much. This means that, when . . . under optimum conditions, three functions (of the personality) become conscious, this has the effect of, also, changing the basic structure of the psyche.

If the unconscious builds up a field of consciousness, the repercussion of such a change produces an alteration in the unconscious structure, as well.

The more they are connected to consciousness, the more they tend to become three good gods and one evil god." [014]

~ Marie-Louise von Franz

This restructuring of the psyche and the ascent of the **fourth** may be understood as Nietzsche's "Overman."

"An Overman ... is the one who is willing to risk all for the sake of the enhancement of humanity ... contrary to the man whose sole desire is his own comfort and is incapable of creating anything beyond oneself in any form. This should suggest that an Overman is someone who can establish his own values as the world in which others live their lives ... an Overman can affect and influence the lives of others. In other words, an Overman has his own values, independent of others, which affects and dominates others lives that may not have predetermined values but only herd instinct. An Overman is, then, someone who has a life ... not merely to live each day with no meaning ... but with the purpose for humanity.

In Nietzsche's view, an Overman should be able to affect history indefinitely." [015]

Nietzsche was one of Jung's greatest inspirations, [016] so it comes as no surprise that within Jung's fourfold structure of the personality, there is room for an Overman; even if we are unable to decide if he is a messiah or a devil.

"Urd, Verdandi, and Skuld stand behind the natural flow of time, which is cyclic, and weave its strands into a pattern, while the fourth function (the Emperor archetype) becomes conscious and emerges from the vicious cycle and lifts itself onto a higher plane of consciousness."

~ Hallfríður J. Ragnheiðardóttir

Creating a New Set of Values

Self-knowledge is the foundation of Self-control. *Know Thyself* was inscribed in the forecourt of the *Temple of Apollo* at Delhi, in Ancient

Greece, taken from an earlier inscription at Luxor Temple, Egypt—the original mystery school. And just what was this mystery?

"There exists no art that isn't religious.
There exists no religion that isn't philosophical.
There exists no philosophy that isn't scientific.
There exists no science that isn't art." #017

Ancient gods were symbolic expressions of psyche and personifications of natural laws. From this duality emerged mysticism (empowerment). Greeks in Hellenistic Egypt (Ptolemaic Kingdom) attempted to contain mysticism as Hermeticism, inspiring the Romans in their creation of modern religion (powerlessness).

Within a century from now, civilization will look back at religion (and much of philosophy, art, and science) as weapons of propaganda used by the ruling elite to maintain control of people who were willing to be told what to think, instead of to think for themselves.

While each of these (art, philosophy, science) pursuits *may have had* noble beginnings, ego transforms these tools into weapons. They have become distractions, keeping consciousness wandering in the shadows of our conceptions. These *shadows of conceptions* are belief systems.

Working our way out of belief systems is at the root of depth psychology. Working our way into alternate beliefs is the messiah/devil lurking within the roots of our greatest imagination.

"When your mind is preoccupied, your impulses, not your long-term goals, will guide your choices." #005

~ Kelly McGonigal

Nietzsche realized the search for God would become absurd. He speculated that the greatest threat to society would be the absence of values, because values give us meaning, which, in turn, gives us purpose.

"A belief structure orients us to action. The presupposition of movement is that where we are moving towards is better than where we have been. We cannot progress without a value structure." [#003]

~ Jordan B. Peterson

In response to the collapse of religion and the death of (the concept of) God, Nietzsche hypothesized that people would either continue to embrace absolutes, regardless of facts and with great fundamentalist fervor, or people would be reduced to their most primal instincts—violence and sexuality.

Alternately, Nietzsche proposed his concept of an Overman, in which humanity realizes their inherent capacity to create *value and meaning* independent of illusion/belief systems.

Progress, in contrast to evolution, is the result of observation. Science is, fundamentally, organized observation. Absolutists are as common within the scientific community as they are within the religious, philosophical, and artistic communities. If we want to facilitate harmony between progress and evolution (biological and cognitive), we must remain teachable. From this, a greater consciousness (than presently exists) will emerge. Absolutes are conceptual boxes. Truth and consciousness will not be so contained.

During the Renaissance, there was a surge in esoteric thinking, including alchemy (of which Jung was fascinated), although hermetic texts ultimately became the folklore of secret societies. The foundation of this knowledge is predicated on the idea that all the principles of nature are reflected within our bodies. Synchronizing this dualistic nature of our physical (symbolic) and natural (logical) environment allows us to transcend right brain/left brain thinking, facilitating the transformation of consciousness into the material universe.

Conclusion

All behaviour is a reaction or response to how we feel about the past, the future, and the present. Intentionally making the effort to identify the impulses provoking our choices allows us to become aware of inharmony within our triune mind. To *know thyself*, we must become consistent observers of our experience *and* the experience of others, while remaining unbiased and non-judgemental. This will allow for a fourth perceptual awareness to emerge, which may be described as an awareness of consciousness as distinct from Self.

Beyond the fourth, we may eventually discover the experience of observing consciousness, but let's not get ahead of ourselves.

First perceptual - Through your own eyes (ego).
Second perceptual - Through the eyes of another (Anima//Animus).
Third perceptual - Observing; bird's-eye view (Self).
Fourth perceptual - Consciousness; detached observation.

Pleasure and gratification often originate in memories of the past or conceptions of the future and are thus, not necessarily, reflective of our ideal state. Recognition of habitual *qualities of behaviour* leads to empowerment.

The Three Norns weave a default destiny—a destiny that will unfold if we take no incentive to become participants in this journey towards Self-realization. Our willingness to discard assumption, restructure priorities, and adjust behaviour to support our ideal state liberates us from the cycle of time they weave.

"The Christian myth is a myth in the real sense of the word."

~ Laurens van der Post

TVÍSKIPTUR

2

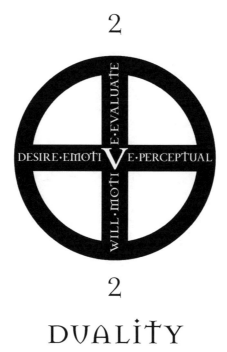

2

DUALITY

"Ancient history for European philosophers was like 500-2000 years ago and Jung thought way past that . . . and started to take into serious account the fact that . . . the origins of our psyche, the ground of our psyche, is deeply biological, and that it's an emergent property."

~ Jordan B. Peterson

"Thanks to the architecture of the modern human brain, we each have multiple selves that compete for control of our thoughts, feelings, and actions. Every willpower challenge is a battle among these different versions of ourselves."

~ Kelly McGonigal

"It would be in no way possible to portray the Being. It resembles an army of innocent children; each of them performs specific tasks. The greatest longing of all initiates is to unify all parts of the Being."

~ Samael Aun Weor

"Above all, it is fair to say we are now beginning to understand better the true meaning of the myth because of the grave strides made in psychology and the study of the human mind."

~ H.R. Ellis Davidson

The **unconscious** or *Universal Mind*, is static, creative potential and contains templates of experience, universal to all of humanity. **Archetypes** represent these behaviour impulses, personified as deities throughout mythology. Each archetype contains a **shadow**, which is, essentially, a repressed expression. A **complex** is a collection of behaviours associated with an archetype/impulse (Thor/War, Dionysus/Inebriation). **Psyche** is the home (Asgard/Olympus) of the gods/archetypes. **Animus** refers to the masculine/Yang characteristics inherent within females and is the *archetype of consciousness*. **Anima** refers to the feminine/Yin characteristics inherent within man and is the *archetype of the unconscious*. The terms Anima and Animus are Jungian terms that refer to *qualities of behaviour* within specific biological systems.

Self is an *archetype of being* and contains the essence of unique experience; the "I" of identity. **Ego** has emerged from the unconscious as an ambassador to the physical world. Without ego, Self would have no idea how to relate to the objective world, which is why we spend the first forty years of life developing ego. Ego may also be understood as the emasculated ruler of the internal pantheon/archetypes.

"Zeus was the most powerful... but he was not all-powerful, because he needed and craved the company of his own family. For that reason, like all patriarchs, he had to settle for an uneasy compromise between power and comfort. Seated on Mount Olympus, he ruled over the entire world, but on the sacred mountain, itself, his family constantly undermined his authority." [018]

~ Barbara Graziosi

Individuation (to *know thyself*) is an emerging conscious awareness of the process whereby unconscious impulses/archetypes compete for our attention. That which holds our attention controls our behaviour. Personal power is our ability to adjust our behaviour to support an ideal state.

"Once the ego has reached a level of development, it does not have to continue this repetitive cycle, at least, not in the same way. The cycle is then replaced by a, more or less, conscious dialogue between ego and the Self." [019]

~ Edward F. Edinger

Sustained harmony between ego, the unconscious, and conscious archetypes will result in **The Transcendent Function**.

"The tendencies of the conscious and the unconscious are the two factors that, together, make up the transcendent function. It is called 'transcendent' because it makes the transition from one attitude to another organically possible." [020]

~ Carl Jung

To facilitate making the unconscious, conscious (Individuation), Jung placed great emphasis on cultivating the relationship with the unconscious through dream analysis, creative expression, and free association.

We must be able to identify the "voices" of dominant archetypes competing for our attention and distinguish them from ego, Self, and our contrasexual (Anima//Animus).

As ambassador to the physical world, ego enables us to become aware of unconscious archetypes, so that we may integrate their intended contribution towards *whole personality development* into our conscious experience.

Creativity is a tool by which we may bring the unconscious (Anima) into consciousness (Animus). This tool may become a weapon when control of creativity (an expression of Anima) manifests as an expression of ego.

Into the Timestreams

Days before the 2016 American Presidential election, I spent the weekend pacing in my apartment like a caged lion.

My awareness of Individuation was growing in tandem with anxiety regarding who would become the next commander-in-chief of the United States. This unconscious anxiety became conscious as *apocalyptic dialogue*—a distress signal sending "worst case scenario" messages from deep within my unconscious to my ego in a coup d'état designed to trigger a fight-or-flight impulse.

The more I reflected on the impact of *apocalyptic dialogue*, the more I wanted out. A sickly romance had developed between us, rooted deep in belief systems that saw destruction as an inevitability. I had become increasingly isolated, justifying this alienation as a cleverly strategic means to achieve unfulfilled ambition. Echoes of this dialogue resounded in empty halls left vacant by incubated estrangement. To put it mildly, I was humbled.

I pushed forward through this imagined future.

As an observer, I was able to see how *apocalyptic dialogue* had manipulated and influenced me for years. It developed in childhood and was encouraged by dogmatic embellishments.

From deep within my unconscious—where it had survived and thrived like diseased bacteria—fear burst forth into conscious expression.

"The fight-or-flight response wants to make you more impulsive... (it is) the built-in ability of your body and brain to devote all... energy to saving your butt in an emergency. You aren't going to waste energy—physical or mental—on anything that doesn't help you survive the immediate crisis... Mental energy that was focused on finding dinner or planning your next great cave painting is re-channeled into present-moment vigilance and rapid action. In other words, fight-or-flight stress response is an emergency management instinct. It decides how you are going to spend your limited physical and mental energy." [#005]

~ Kelly McGonigal

That night I had a dream;

I am facing my mother. Her mouth is sewn closed, despite the fact that she has just spoken. "You have betrayed me," I answer, as I run from the room and into an alley to the exact position where a small camper trailer was parked. It is not here anymore. I try to see into the garage that backs onto the alley, reasoning that the owner may have moved it inside. As I do, I notice my wallet resting on the fence. Instinctively, I reach for it and confirm my worst fears—all of my identification is gone!

Panic sets in as I realize what this means. I will have to replace the missing documents and cancel my credit cards. Also, the potential exists that I could be vulnerable to identity theft. This will be a nightmare that could haunt me well into the future, and I don't want to deal with the ongoing worry and fear this will prompt, nor invest the mental energy needed to deal with this tragedy.

Thoughts are like real estate. What we think about takes up space in the cauldron of creation. The archetypes of our internal pantheon—like witches at a Sabbath—take turns stirring this energy about. The inertia of motion creates swells that become tidal waves, altering our course through life, and threatening to plunge us into the depths of unconscious illusion from whence sirens beckon and consciousness sleeps.

Despite all the work I have done, much more will be required. There is no way to not be consumed with this new potential threat and the timing is terrible—though it never could be ideal.

Before logic can discourage me, I intuitively glance to the ground with anticipation of locating remnants of my lost identity. My driver's license appears first, and a few steps beyond that, a credit card.

Like a trail of bread crumbs, I am led out of the alley as I continue to retrieve items of my missing identity in the street-side gutter and along the sidewalk.

The dream was so vivid that it woke me up. I knew something had changed. Something unconscious was in the process of becoming conscious, and decoding the symbols would accelerate the process.

Symbols are the language of the unconscious. Symbols communicate universal concepts—**Elementary Ideas**—without devaluing subjective experience.

By taking incentive to interpret the symbols of the unconscious as they appear in dreams and waking life, we become participants of our unfolding destiny.

After days of intense introspection and personal reflection, I realized that *conceptions that had become belief systems were illegitimate sources of fear*. They are entirely based on fictional stories we tell ourselves that, when triggered, produce **automatic biological reactions** in the body.

Regardless of the election results, our collective journey towards consciousness-awareness would continue.

The next morning, I awoke with a tune in my head. I spent the day writing and recording a song, *Whatever Happens Next (Individuation)*—my response to *apocalypse dialogue*, in which my unconscious fear was transmuted into a tool of Self-realization.

"The degree of harmony we attain in life is determined by our ability to appropriate what we require for our growth from each experience."

~ Charles Haanel

An Insatiable Thirst

Acknowledging the role of *apocalyptic dialogue* was key to unlocking why a part of me seemed intent on sabotaging my creative projects. Within imagination, I was free to fantasize without consequences and without criticism. If my imagination were to materialize in objective form, I would be vulnerable to, and unable to escape, the scrutiny of others. This is the shadow side of (creative) freedom that *apocalyptic dialogue* was forcing me to confront.

Along with trying to protect oneself from criticism, sabotage also comes when the pursuit of a goal outweighs the benefits of completing the goal. These benefits, known as **secondary gain**, may include validation, the attention we receive from others, and/or the *value and meaning* we extract when working towards the completion of a goal.

Once the process is complete, value and meaning must be replaced because *value and meaning derive from the process; they are not the goal*. For this reason, we must think big thoughts. Our immediate goals are merely a contributing factor to the completion of our "big picture" vision. This vision must remain big enough to ensure the overall process (of transformation) continues, long after the immediate goal is complete.

"Art does not need to be perfect, it only needs to start a conversation."

~ Zeljko Matijevic

Our insecurities reflect illusions we have yet to confront.

The "worst case scenario" filter—which prompts a fight-or-flight response (creative sabotage/abandonment)—can alchemically transform from a weapon into a tool, if we recognize, and take advantage of, the opportunity to examine our fantasies and move beyond our illusions into a more grounded and authentic being.

The immobility of living with *apocalyptic dialogue* kept me perpetually dreaming about what I could accomplish in a future free of this ongoing war within. This dualistic nature of psyche is captured throughout mythology as a recognizable pattern involving a displaced original pantheon.

Just as the Olympians of Greek mythology replaced the Titans (of whom Zeus and his brothers were born), the *Æsir (ICE-ear)* replaced the *Vanir (VAN-ear)* as the second Pantheon of Norse mythology.

"The Æsir are the gods and goddesses of social order and of consciousness, while the Vanir are the divinities of nature and wellbeing.

This pantheon, or family, of divine forms gives the individual a pattern of archetypes, which embody the whole of human experience and torrential." [021]

— Edred Thorsson

While the Romans were eager to amalgamate the religious symbology of the cultures they subjugated, when it came to the people of the North, they were more hostile. The Romans were intent on removing all traces of "pagan" (Vanir) spirituality and existence from history.

When you look at the rest of the world, by comparison, we know much more about the cultures and spiritual practices of the "High Civilizations" to the South than we do of our Northern ancestors.

Archeological evidence of Neolithic settlements on the Orkney Islands of Northern Scotland, shows that civilization thrived in the North, revealing a rich cultural legacy, that forged its way into our collective memory by harmonizing itself with the elements of nature that it was both at the mercy of, and dependent upon. From within this context, pantheism (God is everything), animism (God is within objects), and polytheism (many gods) make tremendous sense.

One may wonder if this classical period of nature-oriented spirituality (known as **Seiðr**, in Iceland) was anticipated as some great threat to the overall agenda of the (Roman) empire and the new monotheistic (one god) religion born from its political ashes.

A 1993 excavation of a Mesolithic settlement off the coast of Norway [022], and the ongoing efforts to "bring to the surface" the 18,000-year-old "lost continent" of Doggerland [023]—a continent that once bridged the United Kingdom with Northern Europe (now submerged in the North Sea following the end of the Ice Age)—are sure to give us a greater glimpse into a civilization that history, and the forces that guide our understanding of it, have made such a grand effort to suppress.

Confronting the Shadow

Behaviour may be understood as an expression of universal evolutionary impulses (archetypes). The extent that we rely, depend on, or are controlled by, patterns of expression (complexes), indicates our dependency on these states. If the *quality of behaviour* we exhibit does not support our *ideal state*, then we are facilitating the possession of an archetype. It is only by recognizing the "voice" and/or *quality of behaviour* attached with the archetypal force(s), that we are able to make the unconscious conscious and regain control of the mind and body/vessel by adjusting our behaviour.

Jung's understanding of archetypes was rooted in the Gnostic tradition, as upheld by alchemists through the centuries and, thus, firmly planted in the patriarchal philosophies of monotheism.

Two thousand years before Jung, Plato understood templates of experience as his theory of forms. [024] Plato—along with Socrates before him, and

Aristotle after—provides us with a unique glimpse of the evolution of cognition, as one of the "high civilizations" was in the process of usurping the pantheism of Vanir consciousness and replacing it with the rationalism of the contemporary Western mind.

Monotheism is the default language of cognition (motive), which is **evaluative**, and corresponds with thinking and feeling.

Pantheism is the default language of the unconscious (emotive), which is **perceptual**, and corresponds with intuition and sensation. These two poles of psyche form one of the most universal symbols to transcend cultural and geographical divides; the cross (+).

The **shadow** is composed of qualities of behaviour we do not want to confront, and is typically mismanaged through denial and abuse of Self or others. Excessive denial—whether intentional or deliberate—leads to pathological ignorance. Excessive denial will find a way to project itself in the material world.

"One of the things you might consider, is that, from the Jungian perspective, a lot of the forces the ancient people considered deities, were personified representations of instinctual systems. Well, here's one way of thinking about it, what is older—you, or aggression?" [003]

~ Jordan B. Peterson

Projection is your psyche's digestive system, designed to make denial a prolonged reflection until you are willing to acknowledge it. For this reason, Jung fiercely maintained the importance of acknowledging and confronting shadow. The importance of this confrontational action may be compared to the advantage of a healthy reflux.

A choice to live in blissful ignorance is simply a choice to maintain a holding pattern on your potential to live a life of pure contentment.

"The system that mediates biological aggression in mammals... is tens of millions of years old, and if you think you control it rather than the other way around, you're deluded about your central nature.

Part of it is that you don't control it at all. What happens is, you never go anywhere you need to use it, and so, one of the things that happens to soldiers in war time, for example, is they go somewhere where they could use it, and out it comes, and the consequence of its emergence is so traumatic that they develop post-traumatic stress disorder because they observe themselves doing things that are hyper aggressive; that they could have never imagined someone like them could have manifested." #003

~ Jordan B. Peterson

Confronting your shadow does not mean indulging it. Rather, it may be understood as intentional observation of *qualities of behaviour* that have been, as yet, unable to find healthy expression within psyche.

The ideal state is a harmonious relationship between ego, Self, and Anima//Animus. Ego must facilitate this harmonious relationship between conscious and unconscious states—between Animus/will/evaluative pole (consciousness), and Anima/emotive/perceptual pole (unconscious).

Acknowledging and confronting the object of thought "possessed" by our shadow gives way to awareness—the kind of awareness that allows us to foresee the consequences of acting on impulses in an unhealthy way. We may, then, adjust your behaviour to a more strategic, healthy expression, in line with your ideal state. This is a personal *response*-ability. To neglect this opportunity is to blaspheme the Individuation process and sabotage your own potential to be happy.

Thought contains value. Value contains assigned meaning. Meaning is conveyed through symbol. Symbol represents *quality of behaviour.*

Our impulses towards specific *qualities of behaviour* have a suggested value by society, which we are free to adopt or reject. Regardless of our choice, there will be consequences.

Consequences are the inescapable burden of choice.

Ego Ideology

Ego emerged from the unconscious to communicate our sensory experience of the object-oriented world to Self.

Ego relates to the unconscious through the "language" of Pantheism—a recognition of the divinity of all consciousness and the ability to communicate this creative potential through symbol.

Ego relates to the **object**ive world through sixty-four templates of experience as described in the *I Ching*. These templates may be understood as a collection of archetypes/gods/goddesses (polytheism).

Ego relates sensory information to Self (consciousness) through the "language" of monotheism—the "absolute truth" of our subjective experience/perspective.

Ego relates to the subconscious through habitual behaviour.

Understanding the "languages" operating within psyche will allow us to become a master of our *inner experience* while creating unprecedented and limitless opportunity in the "outside" world of experience.

The degree to which others understand what we communicate reflects the success of ego in maintaining harmony between our motive (monotheism) and emotive (pantheism) poles of psyche. Understanding does not imply agreement. If ego is unable to convince or compel others of the absolute value of its subjective experience, it may concede to Self-doubt, internally, while misdirecting anger, externally—as though an inability to validate subjective experience were as great a threat to personal identity as the Northern tradition was to the sovereignty of Rome.

When we react, instead of respond, it usually indicates that ego is trying to relate to the **object**ive world through monotheism.

"We're all geniuses in our own head."

~ Zeljko Matijevic

Impulses take form as *qualities of behaviour* relevant to our environment and social context. Our *genius voice* (ego) consistently manipulates us into making decisions based on assumptions. We may disregard this impulse, which leads to regression and projection, or we may take the opportunity to acknowledge and confront this impulse. By doing so, we may discover that our tendency to assume originates within a story we have been telling *Self*. This is the genuine source of frustration for ego, as it indicates we have been caught up in illusion, compelling ego to react.

Our "stories" arise from a compulsion towards craving or aversion, which stimulates **rumination**—a state in which we become fixated on the cause and consequences of "problems" instead of solutions.

Sympathy is often a by-product of rumination, and may quickly sabotage integrity if we confuse sympathy for compassion.

Assumptions are birthed from stories we tell ourselves based on memories of the past or projections onto the future. These stories may be understood as internal dialogues/voices of the archetypes, and they offer us an intimate portrait of our internal pantheon.

Predispositions must be identified if we want to move beyond them. They are based on evolutionary and personal experience. The degree of freedom you will experience in life is determined by your willingness to emancipate Self from default behaviours and weave your own unique destiny. To do this, you must take personal *response*-ability for your choices.

"The conscious mind receives its governing tendencies from heredity, which means it is a result of all environments, of all past generations.

We can consciously use all the desirable characteristics with which we have been provided and we can . . . refuse to allow the undesirable ones to manifest." [#008]

~ Charles Haanel

Assumption robs us of opportunity and consistently alters our trajectory, which makes it difficult to make any significant progress. We may identify these assumptions/dialogues with mindful attention towards our *inner experience*.

Learn to distinguish between what you know to be true in the present, from what you assume based on learned (past) experience. Assumption advises us against accepting people at face value. Assumptions, inevitably, result in contained relationships.

Contained Relationships

Contained relationships are typical of workplace relationships. Personal information is superficial and minimal, if it exists at all. This encourages a lack of individual identity, as employees begin to consider themselves part of a machine, with a specific role. The importance of their contribution is elevated by the demands of the role they contribute, motivating employees to do their work because others depend on them. This offers a desperately sought-after validation, which society seems unwilling to bestow arbitrarily. Contained Relationships are **sympathy oriented**.

The shadow side of contained relationships is the risk of sacrificing authenticity to be accepted by other members of the machine. Religious and political institutions, with overwhelming success, rely on this appeal when recruiting.

Uncontained Relationships

Uncontained relationships thrive on exploration of Self. Time is forgotten in the pursuit of authenticity. The most distinctive quality of uncontained relationships is that they are about honesty, mutual growth, *Self*-discovery, and learning. Uncontained relationships are **solution oriented**.

The shadow side of uncontained relationships is egocentricity. If ego holds on to the *feeling* of empowerment without passing this new information to Self, the information cannot be integrated into psyche.

Co-dependent relationships thrive when ego becomes fixated on maintaining an illusion of our ideal state rather than a pursuit of the genuine. Uncontained relationships that become sympathy oriented keep us locked into our illusions and eventually lose their authenticity, reducing our experience to a contained relationship. To avoid this, we must remain teachable, honest (with ourselves and others), and eager to discard assumptions.

Open Monitoring

The **sympathetic system** is the branch of your automatic nervous system responsible for your fight-or-flight (or freeze) impulse. When faced with any kind of threat, the sympathetic system is activated and our senses are finely tuned to our immediate need for survival. The sympathetic system of nerves is the organ of the subconscious mind.

The shadow side of the sympathetic system is that it may activate when we become angry or feel anxious. This means that when we are overwhelmed with the tasks of the day, the sympathetic system is responsible for, and maintains, our ability to react or respond.

Alternately, this energy can be channeled in healthy ways that promote achievement, excitement, and vitality. This opportunity presents itself when we become aware of our tendency to habitually react, and instead, take the incentive to respond.

The sympathetic system is part of the **automatic nervous system**. The decision to respond or react is automatic. It is a default behaviour. **Conscious choice** allows us to modify default impulses, and co-weave our destiny from the "original" template.

The subconscious does not reason and make decisions, it acts. Our ability to become conscious of instinctual systems is our ability to adjust our behaviour to ensure we respond to a situation that does not call for a reaction.

"Seiðus are not at the mercy of consciousness, knowing it as a phenomenon instead of a thing. Simply put, if they do not like a particular consciousness, they change it, for they understand fully how each thought has a result, that nothing is ever lost, ever, and how some similar thoughts create habits or repetitious behaviour." [#085]

~ Yngona Desmond

The fight-or-flight (or freeze) impulse may be understood as a threat response system.

Reactions are usually based on **stories** we have imagined while ruminating. The good news is that recognition of these "stories" can prevent us from acting *as if they have happened.*

Developing a mindfulness practice is a good way to begin cultivating awareness of our stories. Mindfulness teaches us to become aware of sensations without attaching judgement or entertaining thoughts that may arise as a result of our experiences.

In our modern society, where threats are not what they use to be, **Self-criticism** is often at the root of our fight impulse. Once identified, we may activate Self-kindness in response.

Self-isolation is at the root of our flight impulse. Once identified, we may focus our attention on the common humanity we share with others.

Self-absorption is at the root of our freeze impulse. Accountability to others is a great way to keep us ahead of our illusions.

The **parasympathetic system** promotes healing and relaxation. It is the branch of your automatic nervous system responsible for feelings of contentment, safety and connection, and promoting a soothing sense of compassion and well-being.

What I pay attention to affects me emotionally, which affects me physically. Physical sensation affects what I am thinking.

Quality of Behaviour

By the time I reached high school, I had figured out that making friends was easy. People want to be your friend if you are genuinely interested in their lives and listen more than you speak. When I did speak, I would (attempt to) say something profound, which is easier than you might think. Here's how;

Imagine being a conduit, putting others in touch with their authentic Self by listening to what they say and reframing it in a way that appeals to their Self—who now feels heard and included in the conversation. People speak via ego, which reorganizes what Self is trying to express. This reorganization/translation is necessary to convert the monotheistic language of psyche into *qualities of behaviour* that are necessary for effective communication with the **object**ive world. Some of these qualities include: equality, respect, and patience, as well as any other quality you can easily associate with community and nature-oriented values, otherwise understood as matriarchy.

As we learn to genuinely hear what Self is trying to communicate from amidst the chatter of another's ego, we can relay this information back to them in a way they will find profound and meaningful. Semantics, then, becomes a tool to cultivate empathy.

"Jung recognized that the unconscious was far more sophisticated, in many ways, than the conscious parts of your being, and that it guided your adaptation in ways that you didn't understand, and the ways in which it guided your adaptations and structured your understanding were universal, hence biological, and far more sophisticated than a somewhat primordial drive might indicate." [#003]

~ Jordan B. Peterson

"Universal," in the context Jung was referring, may be understood as the Elementary Ideas that unite mythology, also known as the **perennial philosophy**.

In an effort to *know thyself*, it is useful to explore the impact of personal experience and how this shapes unique perspective within the context of a greater worldview (as shaped by family, society, ethnicity, etc.).

Experiences are neutral and subjective. They receive value when we interpret them through filters of judgement, which is a function of the object-oriented ego mind. The default position, from which we judge, is determined by our belief systems, which form **complex** patterns of behaviour.

We filter present experience through rumination (cause and consequence), which is why the present seems so urgent, dramatic, and, ultimately, reverts us into the past or projects us into the future. The past and future are ruled through either nostalgia (utopia) or entanglement (dystopia).

The predisposition of **nostalgia** is positive. It says; *"My past made me who I am today, and I am happy with who I have become."*

The predisposition of **entanglement** [#025] is negative. It says; *"My past limits who I can become, which means I can never be happy."*

How we integrate our past experiences determines how we will project our expectations into the future.

Our poles of psyche may be understood as **motive** (will/solution/ Gnosticism), and **emotive** (desire/sympathy/Existentialism). A healthy dose of both perspectives is necessary to cultivate resonance and harmony between how we relate to ourselves (monotheism), and how we relate to objects/everything else (pantheism and polytheism).

One of the great problems of modern time is that we attempt to relate to the objective world through the language and philosophy of monotheism, which does not work.

In Norse mythology, the icy landscape of **Niflheimr** and the fiery world of **Múspellsheimr** drifted towards one another along the silent chaos of **Ginnungagap** (the yawning void). This is how the Norse concept of cosmos begins.

Psyche (A Road Map)

As we move towards a more informed understanding of psyche, we must acknowledge the inherent masculine qualities within females (**Animus**), and the inherent feminine qualities (**Anima**) within males.

The key to this typology is an understanding that the quality of Self and ego take on the opposite characteristics of either Anima//Animus.

Imagine two lines stretching down from a point on your forehead to the palm of each hand: ∧

Males: *Imagine in your right hand, you are holding ego, and in your left, you hold Anima. At the top of the triangle, on your forehead, is Self.*

Females: *In your right hand, hold Animus; ego is in the left. At the top of the triangle, on your forehead, is Self.*

Now, imagine you are facing a mirror. What you hold in your right hand, appears on the left. What you hold in your left, appears on the right.

Now, imagine you were facing someone of the opposite gender, and you clasped hands, in this position. The male ego holds the female Animus, and the female ego holds the male Anima.

Male Psychology

Psyche is represented in Norse mythology as the Óðinnic Triad—Thor, Týr, and Óðinn.

Ego emerged from the unconscious as a tool for Self to relate to the objective world. As **Thor,** he is the archetype of the divine child, come into existence as a result of the polarity/procreation between consciousness and unconscious.

Ego interprets the unconscious archetypes and projects their influence on the objective world in relation to our understanding of their *significance* (value and meaning). Ego's ability to govern these impulses determines the *conscious emergence of Self.* Ego may be understood as the first perceptual position (right).

Thor may be understood as the high chair tyrant—the undeveloped boy psychology; a reinterpretation of the young Óðinn.

When the high chair tyrant grows up, he becomes **Týr**—the god of law and justice—who has the potential of becoming a great King, Lover, Warrior, and Wizard.

Anima may be understood as feminine characteristics within the male psyche. She represents the original state/pleroma. Anima is an archetype for the unconsciousness, and represents the emotive (desire/sympathy/perceptual) pole of the psyche. She is understood as the second perceptual position—seeing through the eyes of another. She is expressed by matriarchal pantheism—Vanir psychology.

The Vanir are the original gods of Norse mythology. In Greek mythology, these are the Titans.

The word Vanir is literally translated "accustomed," which may be further understood to mean usual, normal, ordinary, typical, or *original state*. We may look back to our ancient hunter-gatherer ancestors as a source of inspiration in regards to the nature-oriented worldview of the Vanir, as interpreted through animism, pantheism, and the mythologies of matriarchal systems, such as those of indigenous people. These perspectives offer us additional insight into what we already know about *Seiðr*—that before the spread of celestial-inspired patriarchal monotheistic values, the foundation of tradition was structured on matriarchal pantheism.

Self is the archetype of consciousness, and represents the motive (will/solution/evaluative) pole of the psyche. It is understood as the third perceptual position—that of an observer. He is represented in mythology as **Týr**.

(Read description of Animus in "Female Psychology," below, for more insight into qualities of behaviour associated with Self.)

Female Psychology

Psyche is represented in Norse mythology as the Freyja Triad—maiden, mother, and crone.

Ego emerged from the unconscious as a tool for Self to relate to the objective world. As **Maiden**, she is the archetypal goddess of the divine child come into existence as a result of the polarity/procreation between consciousness and the unconscious. Ego interprets the archetypes, and its ability to govern these impulses determines the conscious emergence of Self. Ego may be understood as the first perceptual position.

The Maiden may be understood as the undeveloped feminine psychology. When she grows up, she becomes the **Mother**, who has the potential of becoming a great Queen, Lover, Warrior, and Seer.

Animus may be understood as masculine characteristics within the female psyche and represents the second state of cognition. Animus is the archetype of consciousness and represents the motive (will/solution/evaluative) pole of the psyche. He is understood as the second perceptual position—seeing through the eyes of logic, reason, and war—as represented by the high chair tyrant, Thor, and the mature masculine, Tyr.

Animus is expressed by patriarchal/monotheistic—Æsir psychology. The Æsir are the second pantheon of gods in Norse mythology. In Greek mythology, these are the Olympians. Æsir (singular) literally means "the amounts due." The Æsir (plural) becomes "The swells." [026] Æsir, then, indicates debt (singular), and rolling waves that do not break (plural).

The shadow side of the Æsir is the warlike disposition of these second-generation Norse gods, which may be compared to the military-industrial complex; the dominance-oriented, aggressive, capitalist agenda that runs like a background program throughout Western thought.

Self is an archetype for the unconscious, and represents the emotive (desire/sympathy/perceptual) pole of the psyche. It is understood as the third perceptual position—the observer. She is represented by the **Crone** archetype.

(Read description of Anima in "Male psychology," above, for more insight into qualities of behaviour associated with Self.)

A Brief History of (Immature) Patriarchal Values

The shift from matriarchal (unconscious) values to patriarchal (conscious) values was not instantaneous.

Prior to the Cognitive Revolution, our ancestors were hunter-gatherers, motivated by appetite, aggression, and procreation. As the Neolithic Revolution began (around the same time), ego emerged from the unconscious with a patriarchal disposition towards the dominance of the earth (agriculture), animals (domestication), and each other (slavery). Males gradually became aware of their role in procreation, which established the significance of lineage and a departure from matriarchy.

By 7000 BCE, the socialist values of community-oriented nomadic people took on democratic *qualities of behaviour*. Communities/clans gave way to chieftains, city-states, and monarchies.

In 341 BCE, Constantine's sons banned pagan state religious sacrifices throughout the **Roman Empire**, although pagan temples remained open. Fifty years later, Theodosius (379-395 BCE), issued a series of decrees, which banned pagan practices and ceremonies.

The Battle of the Frigidus (394 BCE) was, perhaps, the final attempt at a pagan revival, and by 451 BCE, Marcian enforced the penalty of death on anyone practicing paganism.

The **witch hunts** (15th-18th Centuries) may be understood as a further attempt by the Empire to eradicate pagan spirituality/matriarchal values. The patriarchal system now included an international banking syndicate, which emerged from the dissolution of the **Khazarian Empire** and the establishment of the Florence Banking Renaissance. The banking cartels created and continue to enable the atrocities of war. [027]

In tandem with the industrial revolution came great advancements in science, and great interest and exposure of esoteric and occult (hidden) thinking to the general public. In spite of the monotheistic values that dominate science and esoteric thought, two **World Wars** at the opening of the twentieth century proved a great distraction and succeeded in burying much of this knowledge. These wars created the condition for **Capitalism** to be resurrected from the blueprints of religious and monarchic templates as a political, philosophical, and quasi-theological precedent.

Our personal, political, and religious beliefs may originate on either side of the will/emotive (Anima//Animus) poles. The two-party political systems are a good example of our inability to resolve polarity. Society swings like a pendulum between the two extremes. Each side tends to view the other as irrational and delusional, perpetuating the tendency to disregard new information that threatens the stability of the story we want to believe; a story we depend on for value, purpose, and meaning.

"Extremes are designated by distinctive names, such as light and dark, inside and out, top and bottom, light and dark, good and evil. These are not separate entities but parts or aspects of the whole." [008]

~ Charles Haanel

The End of a Two-Party System

We tend to swing from one extreme to the other after having become disillusioned with the ineffectiveness of either to meet all of our expectations. Animus believes people are fundamentally bad, while Anima sees people as fundamentally good. [028] This struggle for power is represented in mythology as the struggle between the former pantheon and the new; a struggle between feminine (matriarchal/pantheism) and masculine (patriarchal/monotheism) *qualities of behaviour.*

Extremes are the by-product of fear, contempt, and outrage. We become so overwhelmed by what we cannot control that we neglect what we can control. The inability to recognize the value in maintaining equilibrium keeps the pendulum swinging and patterns repeating themselves.

Frustration, guilt, and our propensity for creating illusion will project itself onto objective reality. This may prompt us towards

Self-actualization, or we may reject this new information and push back into a regressive state. [037]

"Dualism (the idea that mind and body are separate) is always tempting because it fits so well with the way our consciousness feels... The separate mind is invented to do the job of being conscious, but there is not satisfactory explanation of how it interacts with the world or the brain—other than by magic." [090]

~ Susan Blackmore

The Two Primary Functions of Ego

1) Ego has emerged from the unconscious to assist consciousness in comprehending and relating to the objective, physical world.

2) Ego has the responsibility to interpret and integrate the archetypes, and their intended lessons, for the development of our "whole" personality.

If ego fails in either task, it becomes emasculated/subservient to Anima// Animus. Thus, the "battle of the sexes" is a projection of an undeveloped psyche.

Individuation *"... requires an ego that can maintain its standpoint in face of the counter position of the unconscious. Both are of equal value. The confrontation between the two generates a tension charged with energy and creates a living, third essence."*

~ Frith Luton

Third Perceptual

The primary function of Self (consciousness) is to observe. Through the ongoing process of Individuation, harmony between our ego/interpreter and Self/observer, may become the primary default behaviour of psyche. When this harmony is established, it is referred to as **The Transcendent**

Function, and becomes the means by which our life is transformed from a series of experiences into a *Living Mythos*. We will explore this *process of creation* in greater detail in Part Three.

"Conscious mind has the faculty of discrimination; it has the power of reasoning. It is the seat of the will and may impress the subconscious.

Conscious mind is reasoning will. Subconscious mind is instinctive desire, the result of past reasoning will.

To impress the subconscious, mentally state what is wanted."

~ Charles Haanel

We "mentally state what is wanted" by arresting the attention of ego from the drama of archetypal impulses and redirecting attention towards facilitating harmonious communication amongst the triune functions of psyche—ego, consciousness (will/evaluative), and unconscious (emotive/perceptual).

Ego is the channel of moderation. Harmonious communication, necessarily, demands equal expression. Reviewing the stages of your life while identifying conditions and events that shaped your personal outlook will help you recognize subconscious predispositions. **Timeline Review** will lay the foundation for the fourth perceptual position. We will explore Timeline Review in more detail in Part Three of *Living Mythos*, as we journey forward into meaning.

Engaging Fantasy or Observing Possibility

What is fantasy but projection into our unknown future; a daydream of our ideal state? As we explore further, let us continue to remain mindful of the fact that mythology is a collection of conceptions, projected as archetypes/gods in a manner that was *culturally relevant to the experience of the people who embraced them.*

Belief systems may be defined as organized dogma. It takes a conscious choice to believe something. **Conceptions** are theoretical. Conceptions offer form, or structure, to thought—like a sticky web, which captures our attention and groups ideas together.

While conceptions *seem to be* fundamental building blocks of thought, they should not be confused with belief systems. **Belief systems** are, inherently, conceptions determined absolute.

Our study of mythology is not an attempt to qualify belief systems. Rather, it is predicated upon an exploration of consciousness—the ultimate disqualifier of dogma.

"Daydreaming is a form of mental dissipation. Imagination is a form of constructive thought, which precedes all constructive action." #008

~ Charles Haanel

What is the difference between a thought and fantasy; between imagination and illusion? Is there a difference?

If fantasy is a by-product of thought, can thought exist independent of fantasy? Is imagination the fantasy of awareness? If so, in what context?

Words are a modern form of symbol. Runes replaced cave paintings when cognition evolved a method of transporting symbol. Language succeeded in demoting the significance of place, which is an important aspect of the earliest pagan religions. It was no longer necessary to make a pilgrimage to the cave if you could have a symbol of the cave/divine within your home, on your body, or even as a spoken verse.

Despite our greatest efforts to create a centralized system of interpretation, words will always be referenced by experience, not definitions. "Converting" another's interpretation to reflect *our* personal experience, is dogma. Consider the following, from *Inner Work: Using Dreams and Imagination for Spiritual Growth*, by Robert A. Johnson:

"Dreaming and the imagination have one special quality in common: their power to convert invisible forms of the unconscious into images that are predictable to the conscious mind.

It is plain foolishness to believe in ready-made, systematic guides to dream interpretation . . . No dream symbol can be separated from the individual who dreams it . . . Every symbol in your dream has a special, individual connotation that belongs to you alone, just as the dream is ultimately yours alone." [#032]

~ Robert A. Johnson

Non-subjective, dogmatic systems include mathematics and music theory. Both represent elaborate conceptions that describe the properties of their respective interests. By virtue of their reliability, they have become collective, objective truths, shared worldwide, regardless of culture, creed, or gender. They are not belief systems because there is not a competing force in nature that offers an alternate, measurably consistent, methodology, in regards to their function.

Natural laws are the basis for esoteric study. The alchemists sought to extract and preserve the consistency of natural law towards objective (gold) and subjective (Self-realization) perfection.

Reviving *Óðr*

Óðinn (OH-din) receives his name from the Old Norse word *Óðr (OH-thur)*— *"a force that causes people to create or perform any of the arts; to pronounce a prophecy; to enter an ecstatic trance, as in shamanism, to produce scholarly works . . . Óðr is a power that overwhelms and infuses one's being to its core, which ousts one's mundane consciousness and turns one into a frenzied, ecstatic vessel for some mysterious, divine agency that is palpably present in the act."* [029]

~ Daniel McCoy

The Greeks gave credit for inspiration to nine daughters of Zeus, collectively referred to as *The Muses*.

"The Muses are the inspirational goddesses of literature, science, and the arts in Greek mythology. They were considered the source of the knowledge embodied in the poetry, lyric songs, and myths that were related orally for centuries in these ancient cultures." [030]

The concept of a creative muse is most familiar in terms of artists, yet we must remain mindful that *Óðr* is not contained within our labels/

conceptions of an "artist." Óðr is a by-product of Self-realization, just as Óðinn is a universal archetype of Self.

"Whatever their social stature, the men and women favoured by Óðinn are distinguished by their intelligence, creativity, and competence in the proverbial 'war of all against all.' Whether such people become kings or criminals is mostly a matter of luck.

One of the greatest differences between monotheistic theologies and polytheistic theologies, is that, in the former, God is generally all-knowing, all-powerful, all-loving, etc. Polytheistic gods are none of these things; like any human, tree, or hawk, they are limited by their particularity. For Óðinn, any kind of limitation is something to be overcome by any means necessary, and his actions are carried out within the context of a relentless and ruthless quest for more wisdom, more knowledge, and more power, usually of a magical sort." [031]

~ Daniel McCoy

A Central Living Myth

"History and anthropology teach us that a human society cannot long survive unless its members are psychologically contained within a central living myth. Such a myth provides the individual with a reason for being." [106]

~ Edward F. Edinger

To realize the new living central myth required to proceed into the next aeon, we must revive the essence of *Óðr* as a pantheistic expression of the creative potential inherent within us.

The unconscious contains the background program behind all life. We can literally hack into this program and influence outcomes by becoming aware of how the system works.

Ego emerges from the unconsciousness by age three. The purpose of ego is to help Self relate to the objective world. By age seven, it is now the primary conduit to relay this information.

Ego makes choices based on learned behaviour, heredity, and unconscious archetypes. Archetypes help ego discover meaning in experience. Ego expresses whichever archetype is dominant. The dominant archetype is determined by which one is given more conscious attention. We determine this consciously when thinking.

The content of our thoughts determines what we do, how we feel, and our emotions in response/reaction to what we feel—all of which, in turn, determine our thought. This cyclic nature of thought may be used as a tool or as a weapon against ourselves, depending to what degree we are willing to take initiative to focus on thoughts that support our ideal state.

What we think about is determined by what we feed into the brain. The quality of input will determine the quality of output. All the information you take in throughout the day is influencing your thoughts, which is manipulating your behaviour.

"Default choices" are choices we make with no conscious effort to examine our intentions. We determine the default choices of tomorrow by the conscious choices of today.

"The root word imagination is the Latin word imago, meaning 'image.' The imagination is the image-forming faculty of the mind, the organ that has the power to clothe the beings of the inner world in imagery so that we can see them. The imagination generates the symbols the unconscious uses to express itself.

The psychological function of our capacity for fantasy is to make visible the otherwise invisible dynamics of the unconscious psyche.

When we experience the symbol, we simultaneously experience the complex archetype and the inner psychic entity that is represented by the symbol." [#032] ~ Robert A. Johnson

Archetypes are the first line of communication between the unconscious and the ego. They begin speaking to us through symbol before we are even aware they are at work—in dreams, imagination, and personifying those we encounter in waking life.

The archetypes form our internal pantheon. Ego is unable to rule this pantheon, as Zeus was helpless to control his family of gods. [018] Self is constantly working to compensate for the destructive potential of **ego**centricity, an indication of an undeveloped divine child. As a result, Self may communicate directly with our contrasexual, until such a time that ego is mature enough to facilitate a harmonious relationship with both poles of psyche.

Attention directed towards recognizing what archetypes are projecting into your life will reveal the route that psyche is taking to accomplish Individuation.

Through observation and interpretation of ongoing projections of our unconscious—manifest as symbols in dreams and projected within the people and conditions we encounter in waking life—we may begin to assign value and meaning to these symbols in correspondence with our experience. This initiative allows us to *feel* as though life were unfolding *for* us, not *to* us. By taking this **response**-ability, we become empowered. We become participants in this journey, instead of being surprised by what our belief systems were unable to anticipate.

We avoid this fullness of creative potential by outsourcing the task of **creating** value and meaning to our belief systems. All belief systems will eventually fail because they require a point where learning must cease; when we become closed off to acquiring new knowledge from sources that threaten our bias.

Ego is the thought-processing center of psyche. Ego makes the decision regarding how we direct our attention, and whether we respond or react when we do.

How we direct our attention is a choice determined by ego to utilize evaluative (thinking and feeling) or perceptual (intuition and sensation) *qualities of behaviour.* Attention is inspired by desire. Desire may be determined by pleasure. Pleasure is the shadow of the unconscious.

Inner harmony is achieved when ego engages both Self and Anima//Animus in the decision-making process. This requires big-picture thinking, and requires harmony between our contrasexual and Self.

Learning to recognize the voice of Self, as distinct from ego, is vital in the quest to *know thyself.*

Ego's journey towards establishing harmony between Self and Anima//Animus is reflected throughout mythology as the hero's journey.

A bond of trust must be established between ego (divine child) and Self (Queen/King). When trust is established and harmony is achieved within our triune psyche, ego becomes the tool it was intended to be—an active conduit by which motive and emotive poles harmoniously channel energy to and from ego-oriented, objective experience.

"Once the unconscious content has been given form and the meaning of the formulation is understood, the question arises as to how the ego will relate to this position, and how the ego and the unconscious are to come to terms . . . At this stage, it is no longer the unconscious that takes the lead, but the ego." [020]

~ Carl Jung

When we *intentionally* replace the unconscious archetypal narratives with conscious narratives, we will be in a better position to understand and integrate the lessons of the archetypes. Our ability to think is our **response**-ability to participate and co-weave our destiny.

"The process whereby a series of psychic contents—complexes and archetypical images—make connection with an ego and thereby generate the psychic substance of consciousness is called the process of Individuation." [035]

~ Edward F. Edinger

Synchronizing the triune brain (Self, Anima//Animus, ego) is like getting the members of a team to agree on the same strategy.

This results in a realization of psyche as an expression of consciousness.

Self is to consciousness, what bottled ocean water is to the ocean. Individuation is the process of making the unconscious, conscious.

Cultivating a Fourth Perceptual Position

Imagine you are back in the movie theatre. This time, you are sitting up in the projection booth. About fifteen minutes into the film, you notice some children running down the aisle towards their seats. Fifteen minutes later, you notice someone turn around and confront the father of these children. They seem to be exchanging words and then both stand to their feet. At that moment, you see someone about nine rows behind this commotion. It seems this person has been watching the whole scenario and may try to intervene. Looking closer, you are surprised to discover that the person nine rows back is you!

Simultaneously, you understand that you are also the individual who is now punching the father, *and* you are the child watching yourself punch your father.

The result of creating harmony between ego, Self, and Anima//Animus is a restructuring of the psyche, and the emergence of a fourth personality. Jung called the ongoing process of Individuation, **The Transcendent Function.** Nietzsche identified this *quality of behaviour* as a necessary function of the **Overman.**

> *"The tendencies of the conscious and the unconscious are the two factors that together make up the transcendent function. It is called transcendent because it makes the transition from one attitude to another organically possible."* [#020]
>
> ~ Carl Jung

Cultivating a fourth perceptual position is the ability to observe Self, ego, and Anima//Animus all in relation to one another.

Let's do a quick review. As we do, take a moment to visualize each of these perceptual positions.

First - Seeing through my own eyes (ego)

Remember what it was like to be seated directly in front of the children.

The first perceptual position is completely wrapped up in ego. Ego has the potential to limit and/or reduce our experience.

Have you ever wondered if others see you the way you see yourself? It is doubtful.

Consciousness is filtered through subjective personal experience—a function of individual ego.

Second - Seeing through the eyes of another (Anima//Animus)

Recall the experience of being a child.

The ability to see through the eyes of another is the basis for the existence of all archetypal images, originating from within the unconscious.

Take the opportunity to see yourself through the eyes of another person. Do not just think/consider about it, but imagine you are looking at yourself through the eyes of another person—someone you know and interact with, and, then, someone you barely know. Does this change how you see yourself?

Third - Observation of first and second perceptual (Self)

You are now seated nine rows back. Observe.

The ability to observe and distinguish your perspective from another gives you the opportunity to compare and contrast why these perspectives are different, which often leads to a unique third perceptual perspective of a situation.

Consider an opinion you feel confident in expressing—something you feel is truth. Now take the opportunity to consider it from another's point of view. Try to understand the reasons *their* opinion makes *as much sense* to them as yours does to you. Create a dialogue between both perspectives to explore the issue further.

Fourth - Observe Self, Observing (Overman)

Seated in the projection booth, become aware of Self observing the drama unfolding between ego and Anima//Animus.

Self is contemplating how to intervene in a way that would introduce value and meaning to the situation.

Pick a situation from your life to examine. There must be at least one other person in this "scene." Re-experience the scene in its entirety, as though you were experiencing it, again.

Now, rewind the scene, and experience it as the second character in the scene.

Rewind it again and watch the scene projected on the screen at the front of the theatre.

Lastly, from your position in the projection booth, observe all three perceptual positions. Replay the scene. Watch Self, seated in the chair below, harmonize with the first and second perceptual perspectives. Be sure that Self indicates to you in some way, when they have completed this harmonization.

Shapeshifters: Lurking in Our Shadow

Shapeshifting persists throughout mythology [036] as an archetype for deceit. The Norse myths are full of these references. Loki—arguably Óðinn's shadow—was, by far, the master; frequently turning himself into animals and women. The goddess Freyja had a cloak of falcon feathers by which she could conceal herself and take on a false appearance.

Co-dependent relationships are the result of two people meeting (an illusion of) their needs in one another by virtue of their inability to meet these needs in an, otherwise, healthy way. This happens as easily between Anima//Animus and ego as it does between the sexes. In fact, the living archetypes that surround us are projections of this internal friction.

Freyja is one of the most beloved deities of the Norse pantheon. Her story provides us with incredible insight into understanding Anima and the darker impulse that lurks within its shadows.

As one of the original Vanir pantheon that came to be living among the Æsir, it was Freyja who taught the Æsir about Vanir magic, **Seiðr**. Specifically, she instructed Óðinn in these arts and while he was a powerful leader, he was also ridiculed as effeminate for possessing this knowledge.

It is said that Freyja wanders through the nine worlds under assumed identities, searching for her husband, *Óðr*, who is consistently absent, weeping tears of red gold.

"Her husband, named Óðr in late Old Norse literature, is certainly none other than Óðinn, and, accordingly, Freyja is ultimately identical with Óðinn's wife Friggé." [033]

~ Daniel McCoy

Shapeshifters remind me of the sirens of Greek mythology, who lured sailors to steer their ships onto rocks by charming them with beautiful songs.

"Their song, though irresistibly sweet, was no less sad than sweet, and lapped both body and soul in a fatal lethargy, the forerunner of death and corruption." [#038]

~ Walter Copeland Perry

The sirens were Muses of the underworld. They were the companions of Persephone (Freyja/Venus) and continually called on the goddess with their song. In Greek art, they were represented as birds.

Once sailors were lured to their impending death, the sirens would escort them to hell, where Persephone resided six months of the year, following her abduction by Hades.

When I was five years old, my family joined with another for a vacation in the semi-arid, desert climate of Southern British Columbia, Canada. Cactus could be found growing in the sun-bleached foothills of the Okanagan Valley; prickly neighbors amidst orchards and wineries.

One morning, we set off for the beach. As soon as I was able, I wandered away from the group with a small collection of beach toys and made haste to claim territory in the biggest natural sandbox I had ever seen.

I could still hear my parents from where I planted myself, which was a negotiated and acceptable range. I can't say how long I was sitting there when I became aware of a snake, skimming along the surface of the water. I remember watching it, and thinking that I hoped it would not notice me watching. Then, it turned towards me, *as if overhearing what I was thinking*, and began swimming towards land. It slithered off the water and onto the beach in my direction. I was completely paralyzed with fright. When it was about five feet away, it stopped and lifted itself, so that the front half of its body seemed to be standing erect.

Time ceased to exist. I can't even be certain who was charming who.

The next thing I remember is watching it glide back to the water. I arose quickly, abandoning my toys, and ran as fast as I could to tell anyone who would listen.

"Venus is the god of love; actually, of sexual attraction. More particularly, of sexual possession, which is even a better way of thinking about it. And, you might say, 'Why would people conceptualize of those phenomena as gods?'

Well, if you fall in love with someone . . . is that a choice? It doesn't look like a choice. If it's a choice, it's often an incredibly Self-destructive and an idiotic choice, and it's often one that ruins people's entire lives. It's more like a state of possession. And then you might say, 'Well, possession by what?'

Well, it's a dynamic living system, and it's also immortal, in some sense, which is another reason why conceptualizing it as a deity makes sense.

The phenomenon of love, which is a manifestation of a complex biological system, will be around long after you're gone, and was there long before you showed up. And when it manifests itself, so to speak, within you, you're possessed by it, and you do its bidding. And you may do its bidding despite what you most deeply want." [#003]

~ Jordan B. Peterson

All relationships are a projection of archetypes. Our ability to recognize this allows us to consciously participate in the unfolding drama and understand the corresponding, intended lesson. Suffering is a result of unconscious participation, which leaves us feeling helpless and overwhelmed by what we did not anticipate.

Life is fluid, and, as such, we must be as well. Belief systems make this difficult and keep us trapped in conceptions that may once have been necessary, but may now be discarded.

When you were a child, you may not have been permitted to cross the street by yourself or play outside after dark, but as an adult, you refine the standards that were, formerly, necessary to maintain.

Our conceptions reflect a stage in our life and must be revised and updated regularly. We tend to cling to past conceptions and form belief systems because they offer us the illusion of stability and control.

The message of the shapeshifters is to **be aware of distractions, as they are often rooted in deception, and seek to lead us further from our ideal state.**

Most scholars conclude that Freyja's absent husband was Óðinn, who preferred to wander the nine worlds with his ravens and wolves in search of knowledge. The two lovers seemed only to encounter one another on the battlefield, where they collected the dead.

By the time of the Christianization of Northern myth, the battle between the original Vanir pantheon and the Æsir was long over. The mighty war gods—popularized as the totems of Viking raids—had also begun to change.

The days of a young and eager warrior god who killed Ymir, ruled Asgard, and fed only on wine, were long over.

Óðinn had sacrificed an eye to the ancient being, Mímir, for a drink from the waters of wisdom at the well of destiny. He hung upside down from Yggdrasil for the secret of the Runes, and he learned the ways of Seiðr from Freyja. Óðinn was now a wanderer, a figure not unlike Gandalf from *The Lord of the Rings*. Freyja spent most of her time wandering Midgard (earth), looking for her husband. She was welcomed wherever she visited, honoured as a fertility goddess among the people.

While Óðinn is temporarily exiled from Asgard, Freyja sleeps with both of Óðinn's brothers, Vili and Vé.

The inspiration to judge Freyja's behaviour as infidelity Is the result of the influence of Christianity upon Norse mythology. In truth, Vili and Vé are simply another version of the Óðinnic Triad. In this version, Óðinn first appears as the giant slayer and creator of the world (father), then the Warrior King of Asgard (son), and finally, as the wanderer (Holy Spirit).

Keep in mind that there was no centralized Norse system, so we have multifaceted myths to contend with from regions scattered across Northern Europe.

In the Christianized canon of Norse mythology, any attempt to unite the distinct narratives of Óðinn's timeline are dismissed, as if a deliberate effort is taken to highlight *qualities of behaviour* in support of a revised Óðinnic Triad—one that supports the agenda of a Christianized war machine.

In his final form, all the gods seem to have lost track of wandering (fourth perceptual position) Óðinn. He consistently appears on the battlefield, to collect half of the fallen warriors to escort to Valhalla where they train for the great battle of Ragnarök—the end of the gods.

Freyja claims half of the "weapon dead" and takes them to her hall at Folkvang, or "field of the people." This seems to be the only time the separated lovers are reunited.

The fractured relationship between Freyja and Óðinn symbolizes a disharmonious psyche, in which ego has not yet matured into its role as the great equalizer.

As high chair tyrant (Thor), immature ego attempts to identify with either Self or our contrasexual, instead of facilitating harmony between both. As a result, promiscuous Anima seeks validation from ego, which encourages Self to embody the qualities of behaviour we associate with the wicked stepmother or domineering father archetype.

Confronting and liberating ourselves from our attempts to live up to the impossible standards of the domineering father or wicked stepmother is essential to the maturation of ego from high chair tyrant to emancipated facilitator of harmony.

In the Genesis story, Eve earns mans resentment for acquiring knowledge at the expense of sacrifice. There is no longer harmony in the "garden" because man has become aware of his ignorance (nakedness), and must toil (work) in order to acquire food and clothing (knowledge). Knowledge is symbolic of consciousness. Unanticipated change stimulates resentment because it leaves us feeling powerless—as though life were happening *to* us, not *for* us. We are responsible for our knowledge and our ignorance, and this response-ability is the foundation for the "battle of the sexes."

It's as though men would rather kill the messenger than take initiative to use their newfound ignorance to better themselves.

Willpower: A Shapeshifter's Greatest Enemy

Following the Æsir-Vanir war, the walls of Asgard were in ruin and a giant came by offering to repair the wall in exchange for Freyja's hand in marriage *and* the inheritance of Sun and Moon. The significance of this inheritance would lead to the beginning of Ragnarök.

The gods agree to this arrangement, because they believe the task is impossible to complete in the agreed-upon time.

As the deadline approaches, it became apparent that the giant will accomplish the task, so Loki transforms into a beautiful stallion and seductively lures away the giant's horse, which has been transporting the heavy stone used to rebuild the wall. As a result, the giant is unable to finish the rebuild in time and defaults on their arrangement. Loki is celebrated for his deception.

Ironically, Loki (Óðinn's shadow) is the father of Fenrir, the great wolf who will be released at Ragnarök and will consume creation. Either Loki/Óðinn is not yet ready for the end of days, or he just prefers to be the instigator.

Relationships must be regularly examined to ensure they are supporting our ideal state. If left unmonitored, relationships can become co-dependent and create **relational belief systems (RBS)**. Relational belief systems are created when value and meaning originate from, and depend upon, our relationship(s).

Relational belief systems encourage co-dependency and undermine our creative potential, which makes us vulnerable to the moods and whims of another.

We must discover value and meaning autonomously—from within our unique experience. Relationships and conditions in life are temporal. They are beyond our ability to consciously control and exceed our **response**-ability.

It is not our business to control the experience of others, nor does it serve our greatest potential to allow others to control our experience.

Distractions create the conditions for co-dependency and RBS. Self-control is intimately linked with intention.

Whatever Happens Next

The more we resist change, the harder transition becomes. Making the unconscious, conscious is the method by which we alchemically transform anxiety into transcendence and realize our inherent immortality. Telling ourselves (and one another) that fear-based, worst case scenario stories will only cause *the swells* of emotion that lead to tidal waves of assumption.

The following Taoist parable well-illustrates this;

There was an old farmer who had laboured many years. One day his horse ran away, and, upon hearing the news, he was visited by his neighbours. "How terrible that this has befallen you," they exclaimed!

"I do not know if this is a good or bad thing," the farmer replied. The next day, the horse returned with three wild horses. Upon hearing the news, his neighbours visited again. "How wonderful this has happened," to which the farmer replied, "I do not know if this is a good or bad thing."

A few days later, his son tried to break in one of the wild horses and was thrown from the horse. He broke his leg and was unable to help his father in the fields. Upon hearing the news, his neighbours, again, visited the old farmer and repeated their original refrain, "How terrible that this has befallen you," to which the farmer, again, replied, "I do not know if this is a good or bad thing."

The next day, military officials arrived at the village to draft young men. Upon seeing the farmer's son had a broken leg, they passed him by. The villagers—mourning the loss of their sons to conscription—came to the old farmer and said, "How lucky you are that your son fell from his horse and broke his leg, as he does not have to go off to war." The old farmer replied, "I do not know if this is a good or bad thing."

Each of us is a *living mythos*. Our experience of the world is predicated on the conceptions that form our chosen methodological worldview. Memories are shared experiences—separate and distinct perspectives of a single event.

Why do we settle with conceptions instead of acknowledging what we don't know? What is our current role in evolution?

The cognitive revolution never ended. As consciousness continues to emerge, what form will it take? Will it be as dramatic as the events that allowed next-generation Homo sapiens to wipe out Neanderthals?

Mythology provides a context we may use to assist us in understanding our experience.

Every belief system we have is a conception we are projecting onto the world. The reason we are in conflict with one another is because we are not sharing a conscious experience. Instead, we are comparing whose experience deserves more envy. When we discover how to facilitate a mutual experience of consciousness, we will step into a new state of awareness that spirituality considers transcendence. There will be no need for politics or religion. Both are conceptions rigidly framing reality in a context of borders and limitations.

Moving forward, here are some things to keep in mind:

1) Thoughts are conceptions.

2) Conceptions become belief systems when considered absolute.

3) All belief systems produce dogma.

4) All dogma is propaganda.

5) Propaganda thrives on illusion.

If we want to rise above outdated, failed attempts at Self-rule, we must allow consciousness to restore harmonious balance between the triune functions of psyche and facilitate the fourth perceptual perspective needed to navigate the timestreams of experience.

Ego's resistance to this is the "rebellion", which perpetuates the "fall of man" from the heavenly "ideal state" of Eden into a world of conceptual borders and obstacles, which give form to objective experience.

Ego has, quite successfully, become the master of our reality, regardless of the quality of job it is doing.

By allowing ourselves to fall further and further into our conceptions, we have created belief systems, which are the source of prolonged suffering for ourselves, as we tighten the harness around our expanding universe/consciousness.

The Norse god, Týr, loses his hand after placing a collar around Fenrir, son of Loki—the great wolf who will be released at Ragnarök.

Progress is not meant to be contained in a glass jar of logical conceptions/belief systems. If we are not careful, we may end up like Týr, and lose our ability to fight back. At worst, we will suffer greatly before our inevitable annihilation. At best, we will destroy ourselves quickly in a gluttonous attempt to make the next big bang more elaborate than the one that happened thirteen billion years ago (which we still can't explain).

There is only one alternative to these options. When we choose to respond instead of react, we draw the consciousness out of people. This choice is the foundation of love. Love is the key to evolution.

When the Norse gods grew weary of their war, they agreed to end it on terms that sent two of the Æsir to live with the Vanir, and two of the Vanir to live among the Æsir.

Njorn and his son, Freyr, were the two Vanir appointed to Asgard. Freyja—the twin sister of Freyr—joined them, and together as a Triad, they immigrated to the Æsir pantheon.

"Most metaphysics today argue that both possibilities can be encountered—and are encountered—in many religions: that the soul at its final stage can chose to melt with the One (the pleroma), or maintain its separate identity inside the One (Individuation)."

~ C.G. Jung

Resolving Illusions

No matter how much you may want to believe it, the hero's journey will never be about rescuing the princess, nor will the princess have need of rescue from anyone but herself.

Both the hero and the princess must journey forward, having redeemed one another from the expectations of the other.

The Freyja Triad - maiden, mother, and crone offer us insight into the journey Anima must experience to become a fully-realized version of the emotive/perceptual pole of psyche.

The Óðinnic Triad - Wōden, Vili, and Vé offer us insight into the journey Animus must experience to become a fully-realized version of the motive/evaluative pole of psyche.

At best, we will be inspired to see a bit of ourselves in one another. At the very least, we will achieve some clarity in respect to how we relate to our own duality.

The wicked stepmother stands shoulder to shoulder with the overbearing father, as our hero's journey is about to begin.

"We are most alone when we are with the myths."

~ Alexander the Great

ÞÝÐIR

3

3

MEANING

"People will do anything, no matter how absurd, in order to avoid facing their own soul. One does not become enlightened by imagining figures of light, but by making the darkness conscious."

~ Carl Jung

"A good way to connect to the inner parts of yourself is to think of each dream figure as an actual person living inside you. Think of each person in your dream as one of the autonomous personalities that coexist within your psyche and combine to make up your total Self. It is best if we get acquainted with our inner personalities as persons in their own right before we start putting distance between us and them by using psychological classifications and jargon."

~ Robert A. Johnson

"Jung was able to point out that to the degree that you condemn others and find evil in others, you are, to that degree, unconscious of the same thing in yourself, or, at least of the potentiality of it. There are people who are unconscious of their own dark side, and they project that darkness outwards and they say, 'There is the darkness and it is not in me. I am justified.' But to the degree that an individual becomes conscious that the evil is as much in himself as the other, to this same degree they are not likely to project it onto others."

~ Alan Watts

When I was six years old, my teenage uncle snuck out of his basement window one evening and went to the river with alcohol and some other friends. They climbed to the top of a cliff to feel the excruciating thrill that would accompany plunging into the river below.

The spot they were jumping was familiar to the teenagers, though it was dark out, and they did not account for obstructions in the water.

With the odds so stacked in our favour, one may begin to wonder if unfortunate events are the result of an underlying condition or force. We tend to call this force fate, although our understanding is misdirected when we do. I believe that a more appropriate description of what we are trying to discover may be conjured through an exploration of *meaning*.

I have a photograph of myself lying on a hospital bed next to my teenage uncle Rob. Diving from the cliff, his head was first to come in contact with a log that floated silently in the river.

The prognosis was not good. They were giving Rob only a few years to live.

He spent the next six months at the hospital and the rest of his life in a wheelchair. He exceeded their projected life expectancy by nearly twenty-five years, and I have many wonderful memories of spending time with Rob. He spoke to me as though I were his peer, investing in me a passion for learning, questioning, reading, and cultivating imagination. He was an avid gardener and excelled at being able to extract psychology and philosophy from fiction.

"Challenging the meaning of life is the truest expression of the state of being human."

~ Viktor E. Frankl

As we begin to orient ourselves towards a *meaning* tense, we must pause to imagine our experience of compassion. Our understanding—and misunderstanding—of what compassion is, directly impacts the way in which (the conception of) meaning integrates into psyche.

Compassion is one of those loaded words that is, by-and-large, defined subjectively. In other words, each person has a unique understanding of compassion based on their experience—or lack of experience—with *qualities of behaviour* they consider/believe to be compassionate.

Last night I had a dream I was sitting in a chair opposite uncle Rob's hospital bed. We had both aged to reflect my waking experience.

Next to his bed, my grandma hovered, while two of Rob's sisters flanked me on either side. I was emphatically whining to them in regards to someone I knew who had been in an accident and was now a quadriplegic. There was absolutely no irony present, as though it did not even occur to me that Rob was in a similar position.

At some point, Grandma spoke to Rob. "You're going to be late if you don't get a move on," she said. With that, Rob threw back the covers and stood to his feet. He walked to the end of the bed, put on a ball cap, took his lunch bag, and walked out of the room.

Is the Universe Friendly?

I *don't* think compassion is focusing my attention on conditions I am unable to change or influence because another is, has, or could be suffering. For years, I have operated on the assumption that this was, in fact, compassion. [040] Having experienced this unconscious concept, I confronted it and have a revised context for understanding what I believe compassion actually is.

I think compassion is focusing my attention on conditions *I am able* to change or influence because another is, has, or could be suffering.

Did you catch the difference?

Our ability to distinguish compassion from a host of other emotional reactions prevents us from losing ourselves within *the swells* of emotional currents that compete for our attention.

We may begin to consider some habitual lifestyle behaviours we have embraced because we have mistaken compassion for sympathy.

"'What is the thing which above all others you would like to know? If you could ask the Sphinx one question, and only one, what would the question be?' After a moment's silence, Myers replied: 'I think it would be this: Is the universe friendly?'" [041]

~ Emil Carl Wilm

Why would this question, "Is the universe friendly?" hold such importance to anyone?

It is the difference between a universe that works *for* you and one that happens *to* you.

This predominant mental attitude will determine your assumptions, which influence your behaviour, and, in turn, become the object of your thought.

The structure of the unconscious may be adjusted by conscious will. Each conscious thought supports or discourages the current trend we are on. Successive concentrated thought has the power to navigate our movements, like a rudder on a boat.

Learning to control the vessel you inhabit is the essence of Individuation, and *Living Mythos* is a projection of active imagination, designed to liberate the initiate from the collar of conventional belief systems, empowering the individual to create value and meaning that relates to their unique subjective experience.

Assumptions are only as useful as the reliability of our knowledge.

If you have the ability to change or remedy behaviour that does not support your ideal state, and you neglect to do so, you forfeit compassion, as it *in no way* applies to you.

If the universe *is* friendly, it can be trusted. If it is hostile, we spend our life anticipating attack. The conditions we encounter in life will be predicated on our predominant mental attitude. The good news is, we may adjust this by conscious thought. As Schrödinger's cat reminds us, the observer gets to decide.

"A human being is a part of the whole, called by us 'universe,' a part limited in time and space. He experiences himself, his thoughts, and feelings as something separated from the rest of mankind; an optical delusion of his consciousness. This delusion is a kind of prison for us, restricting us to our personal desires and to affection for a few persons

nearest to us. Our task must be to free ourselves from this prison by widening our circle of compassion to embrace all living creatures and the whole nature in its beauty. Nobody is able to achieve this completely, but the striving for such achievement is in itself a part of the liberation and a foundation for inner security." [042]

~ Albert Einstein

To generate the maximum amount of *meaning*, the remaining text has been presented in a nearly identical fashion to my method of delivery during a live presentation.

At any given time, the human experience allows for nine possible dialogues, all competing for our attention. These dialogues may be understood as the archetypes of Lover, Warrior, and Magician. Each of these archetypes are interpreted through the threefold structure of the personality, ego, Self, and Anima//Animus, for a total of nine primary dialogues.

In the pages ahead, you will discover nine challenges that are designed to assist you in bringing the unconscious into consciousness. As you are about to discover, this begins with recognition of nine primary dialogues that determine the destiny of your life. The good news is that once you discover what these nine primary dialogues are, you are free to replace them with new primary dialogues that support your ideal state.

When you arrive at a challenge, I advise you to pause from reading to complete the challenge and *resume only after completion*. This gesture will ensure that you are giving Self the greatest opportunity for empowerment. After all, if you are going to spend the time to read this book, you may as well get everything you can from this experience, right? Choose the optimal experience.

While you may bypass the challenges—even if your intention is to return to them—you will forfeit your opportunity to complete these challenges while remaining curious for what is coming next. *Cultivating curiosity is essential for transformation,* and curiosity trumps contempt.

The degree of empowerment you will receive is exponential if you follow the prescribed format.

Why not make this commitment to yourself official? By signing your name below, you agree to complete the challenges as they arise, before moving forward, and by doing so, agree to maximize your empowerment.

x--

~1~

Are you interested in becoming a master of your destiny? Would you like to create your ideal future, now?

Okay, first things first. Do you have a picture of your ideal future? Can you visualize this?

Let's take a moment to imagine . . . a lemon, inches away from your face. See the rough, outer peel. Imagine slicing into the lemon and observe the sour juices splashing out. Some of the juice is now on your finger and you gently touch your lips, allowing the juice to drip naturally.

Can you smell the scent from the lemon?

You may be thinking how nice it will be to squeeze out some of this juice from the lemon into a glass of water and enjoy it.

Hold this image in your mind for a moment before you proceed.

Good.

Did your mouth water during that visualization? Did your throat get dry? This is a great exercise to practise until you can literally feel your mouth salivating, because fostering a vivid imagination is a major step towards arriving at your ideal destination in life. This exercise also reminds us that our senses can be hijacked by thoughts, which can be a great tool or a destructive weapon as we journey towards maintaining our ideal state.

Cosmos

Within the three roots of the great ash tree, **Yggdrasil**, is the "yawning void" known as **Ginnungagap**.

In Norse mythology, cosmos came into being as the icy world of **Niflheimr** ("Abode of Mist") and the fiery world of **Múspellsheimr**, both stretched into the gaping abyss of Ginnungagap. When they met, the fire melted the ice and produced water.

And so, it was that a new aeon began.

We are given no explanation for the creation of Niflheimr, Múspellsheimr, or of Yggdrasil, for that matter. We can only assume these were the remnants of a previous aeon.

"You may say, 'How could it be that this expanding universe—getting colder and colder, thinner and thinner—suddenly became a very, very, hot, condensed universe?'

Our galaxy is going to collide with another galaxy, the Andromeda galaxy... In the center of our galaxy is a black hole... which is about four million times the mass of our sun... The Andromeda galaxy has one, which is twenty times bigger, maybe forty times bigger. When we collide, they will spiral around and swallow each other up, and when that happens, there will be one huge release of energy. In the aeon before ours, this will have happened." [#043]

— Sir Roger Penrose

Yggdrasil is kept alive by the service of the Three Norns who draw water from **Urðarbrunnr** ("well of fate"), mix it with sand, and apply this paste to the roots and branches of Yggdrasil, so they will not rot.

Óðinn once hung himself from Yggdrasil for nine days and nights. He fasted during this time and wounded himself with his own spear. As a result of this sacrifice, Óðinn gained the knowledge of Runes. In a separate instance, at the "well of fate," Óðinn gouged out one of his eyes and offered it to the mystical being Mímir, in exchange for a for a sip of the "cosmic knowledge" contained within the water.

Just as Óðinn *"sacrificed what we might call his 'lower Self' to his 'higher Self,' so Óðinn did in the tale of his relinquishing an eye: he exchanged a profane, everyday mode of perception, beleaguered with countless petty troubles, for a sacred mode of perception, in which the world reveals itself to be divine, the very flesh of the gods, constantly enacting the stories of which the gods are the actors, shimmering with meaning and wonder."* [044]

~ Daniel McCoy

In addition to Urðarbrunnr, two other wells can be found beneath Yggdrasil. **Hvergelmir**—beneath a root in Niflheimr (fire), and **Mímisbrunnr**—corresponding with Múspellsheimr (ice).

We may understand the three roots of Yggdrasil as corresponding to the three functions of our Triune brain.

Not Somewhere You Want to Be Lost

When I was nineteen, while driving back to LA, we stopped at Joshua Tree National Park. Have you ever been to a desert? It is not somewhere you want to be lost.

In the desert, you must be aware at all times because there are inherent dangers, like rattlesnakes, coyotes, and vultures. The venom weakens you, the coyotes take you down, and the vultures finish you off.

We were talking about this as we parked the van and began our journey into the sunbaked sand.

About thirty minutes later, wouldn't you know it, one member of our group had a close encounter with a rattlesnake. Actually, it turned out to be a snake-looking stick, but this was not realized until he emptied half his water bottle in the direction of the imagined predator. Shortly after this occurred, we realized we were lost, and one of us had almost no water left.

Ok, so now I am going to ask you to get up from where you are sitting and find another place to sit. You will understand and appreciate the relevance of this request as we proceed.

I trust that you have found a new seat. If you are considering dismissing this request, let me remind you that incentive on your part must, necessarily, accompany intention.

As we navigate our way through life, we can become crippled by thoughts, assumptions, and ideas. When this happens, we lose the ability to respond and we often react in a way that is inappropriate to the situation—like when we are overtired. Fatigue gives way to indifference. Anxiety is often a reaction to procrastination and may be understood as a perpetual fight-or-flight experience.

Longest Nights

One of the longest nights of my life was spent in a small tent at the base of a glacier. This was in the Yukon Territory, in Northern Canada.

It was a two-day hike along a river to reach the base of the glacier. Earlier that day, while eating lunch on a hillside, we spotted a grizzly bear on the other side of the river. It was incredible to watch the massive grizzly. When it caught our scent, it tore off running in the opposite direction, easily lunging up the bank of the river, and disappeared into the dense trees.

Imagine an incredible expanse of wilderness. The Yukon is nearly the size of Spain. While the population of Spain is forty-six million, the population of the Yukon is about thirty-three thousand. We had not seen a single person on our hike, so when you are two days from the nearest road, and you see a Grizzly, you realize you are completely on your own.

We See What We've Been Trained to See

Have you ever questioned the behaviour of others? Of course you have. Have you ever tried to actually understand their intentions? Maybe not so much.

While upbringing is not an excuse for behaviour, it does provide a necessary context to understand what motivates people and the challenges they encounter in the process of Individuation.

Religious fanaticism is a good example. I vividly recall the siege at Waco, Texas, in 1993. It began when the ATF showed up at the compound of a religious sect called the Branch Davidians—an offshoot of the Seventh Day Adventist church. The Branch Davidians believed they were living in the "end times," and the sight of armed men storming their property surely would have been a manifestation of exactly what they expected to happen; a confirmation of Adventist theology/eschatology.

It's like seeing pictures in clouds. The reasoning brain is constantly looking for proof to support our understanding of the conditions we encounter in life. This is why it is so important to scrutinize and refine our beliefs. If we never question the stories we tell ourselves, we will be manipulated by the unseen forces of our assumptions, regardless of whether demonstrable truth supports our subjective experience.

"Biblically, we saw in the prophecies that God's people were going to have to fight the enemy—the devil, and people inspired by the devil, would make war on God's people and overcome them and kill them and all this, so—all I can say is that most people in this country have guns." [045]

~ Clive Doyle, Waco Survivor

Genetic Epistemology

Jean Piaget was a psychologist and philosopher. He observed four primary stages of cognitive development. As we briefly look at these four stages, instead of imagining a child, observe *you* as a child from a fourth perceptual position.

Sensory Motor Stage (Birth-2 years)

This stage is defined by **object permanence**. Babies are not sure what happens to objects when they leave their line of sight. Object identification—relating one's Self to the **object**ive world, kickstarts the development of ego.

Pre-Operations Stage (2-7 years)

This stage is defined by **egocentrism** and the inability to understand another's point of view. Logic is not a factor in decision making. Learned behaviour is based on repetition, thus, if something happened a specific way one time, it must, necessarily, happen that way at all times.

For example, short and wide glasses contain the same amount of water. When the water from the short, round glass is poured into a taller, thinner glass, a child in this stage will identify the taller glass as containing more water than the short, wide glass.

Concrete Operational Stage (7-11 years)

This stage is defined by **logical thinking**. Santa and the Easter Bunny are identified as childish deceptions. Subjects are broken down into categories. Symbols are manipulated into form. Ego is challenged by the perceptions of others.

Formal Operational Stage (11-16 years)

This stage is defined by **abstract thinking**, a process that relies on systematic rational thoughts and concepts. Problems can be solved in a variety of ways. Values and moral judgements develop.

"As children, we learn about ourselves and life in a broader sense by observing and listening to others . . . We form beliefs and rely on these to shape our sense of reality . . . Through repetition, others' views eventually become ours by a subconscious process of internalization. Our sustained identification with our acquired views progressively shapes the neural configuration of brain pathways. Repeatedly identifying with the world as it is presented to us also shapes the person we become. As we later discover, a good deal of information we receive from our parents and others happens to be incorrect." [046]

~ Dr. Bruno A. Cayoun

These four stages of development may also be understood to represent the evolution of consciousness, additionally represented by the four perceptual positions.

Challenge 1: First Years

Purpose: The first years of our life can provide the context to understand the origin of unconscious belief systems. Without this awareness, we forfeit the opportunity to replace unsupportive ongoing dialogues.

Tools: Audio Recorder, notepad (optional)

Instructions: Record an audio journal, sharing as much information as you can in regards to the first three years of your life. Where did you live? Who would you have interacted with? Were you healthy? As an observer in your home, what would you experience? Siblings? Pets? Share any memories. If you need to place phone calls to family to gather more info, do so.

* Give yourself extra credit for finding out what was happening in your mother's life while you were in the womb.

Further information regarding childhood cognitive development can be accessed at www.youtube/visceralmfi in the section titled, Cognitive Development.

~2~

Our behaviour during unanticipated events will always indicate our predominant mental attitude, which is a reflection of the nine primary dialogues that compete for our attention.

As you begin to consider your primary dialogues, be mindful of the fact that these are subjects that dominate your thinking consistently throughout the day.

If your primary dialogues support your ideal future, you will find it more natural to maintain your ideal state.

Start making a mental list now. You should be able to identify at least three without much effort at all.

As you consider this, I would ask that you please begin tapping your foot and continue to do so as you read on.

Can you remember ever seeing dried up fruit? I want you to imagine a dried out and shrivelled avocado.

This is how I was beginning to feel, wandering through the desert.

I was not wondering if my girlfriend remembered to water the plants, feed the dog, or if she was planning a special dinner upon my return. My primary concern was survival. This is the function of the fight-or-flight impulse—to keep us alive.

Our ability to respond appropriately is determined by our predominant mental attitude, which is revealed under the spotlight of the primary dialogues that compete for our attention. These are the forces that truly possess us—our thoughts.

Ego/Ymir

Ymir was a primordial giant who came into existence when rime—frozen fog drifting into Ginnungagap from Niflheimr—met with hot air carried into the great void from Múspellsheimr. Ymir is considered the ancestor of all giants who reside in **Jötunheim**.

Ymir (Germanic) emerges from the earlier Indo-European tradition, where Yemo (twin) is the brother of Manu (man).

In the Norse version, Ymir is not a twin; he is a hermaphrodite. From the sweat of his armpits were produced the first (human) male and female.

Óðinn and his two brothers kill Ymir and use his body to create earth. [047]

The significance of a triad [048] is woven throughout worldwide mythology and the religions that evolved from them.

Óðinn has two brothers. Óðinn is the eldest, Vile, the second, and Vé is the youngest. The three brothers' names are alliterating, [049] so they may be taken as forming a triad of *wōdaz (inspiration), wiljô (knowledge), and wīhą (numen/divinity).

"Pluto and Hades differ in character, but they are not distinct figures and share their two major myths. In Greek cosmogony, the god received the rule of the underworld in a three-way division of sovereignty over the world, with his brothers Zeus ruling the Sky and Poseidon the Sea. His central narrative is the abduction of Persephone to be his wife and the queen of his realm." [050]

~ William F. Hansen

Meanwhile, Back in the Desert . . .

Wandering in the desert, I was concentrated on solutions that might lead to survival. I remember thinking that the water I had with me was the most valuable thing on the planet.

There were some other dialogues, like:

-I am lost.

-I have a bit of food, but I am not sure anyone else does.

-We may not be as lost as we think.

-We may be in more trouble than we think.

-Perhaps it was not a good idea to take mushrooms, wander into the desert, and lose eye contact with our vehicle.

-Who in our group is going to freak out first, and what role will I play as the reality of our situation sets in?

There is no Need to Judge Yourself

Are you still tapping your foot? If not, there is no need to judge yourself—just begin again. Only, this time, I would ask that you begin tapping your other foot. No matter what happens, keep tapping your foot. Consider this your most important task. If you stop, it is because your mind is caught up in a dialogue that is neither about the content you are reading, nor the task of tapping your foot. A wandering mind means you are withholding your own empowerment.

As you may have guessed, the purpose of tapping your foot is to occupy one of your primary dialogues. With awareness and intention, you may begin to replace any internal dialogue that does not support your ideal state.

Mind is constantly wandering amidst nine primary dialogues, or any of the other fifty-five measurable human conditions as defined by the *I Ching*. The sixty-four Hexagrams of the *I Ching* may be understood as *qualities of behaviour—archetypal templates* from which we produce the gods and goddesses of our pantheons.

Each has a distinct voice and personality we may learn to identify. These dialogues can be healthy or unhealthy expressions of the options available as a result of our free will.

Mindfulness creates an awareness of our habitual tendencies.

Now, you remember the dried avocado, right?

Can you still visualize the sour juice running down the sides of the lemon and sticky on your lips?

Perfect.

How is your list of nine primary dialogues coming along? One of those dialogues has been replaced by the effort it takes to remain tapping your foot, right? So, you need at least eight other things that have been going through your mind in the last thirty minutes. You do not need to identify the archetype, only consider the topics you have been thinking about—sex, family, a project you need to complete at work, etc. Begin with identifying the topic of your thought, and then you can more easily identify the archetype from the *quality of behaviour* the thought inspires.

If you are working through this chapter with a partner or a group of people, don't worry, because I am not going to ask you to share your list. Feel free to be honest. Writing, and, even better, speaking aloud, brings a heightened level of awareness in relation to what you think because it becomes a tangible and objective expression. Often, when people *hear* themselves say something out loud, their perspective changes.

What we believe often changes when we hear ourselves speak.

Honesty with Self is, really, the only way to get the most from this experience. Honesty is a precursor to Self-knowledge and is evidence of the incentive required to become a master of your ideal state.

Meanwhile, Back in the Yukon . . .

We made it to the base of the glacier as the sun was going down. By dusk, we pitched our cocoon tent and made dinner.

After a satisfying meal, I walked to a nearby overlook to gaze out at the river we had followed to reach our destination. On the other side of the river—no further from us than it had been at lunch—was the grizzly bear.

We may begin to think of the fight-or-flight impulse as an early precursor to mindfulness, because, when activated, our attention is so captivated by the instinct to survive that we become a true master of our destiny.

Designed to Save Us

The good news about fight-or-flight is that it was designed to save us. Additionally, we have a prefrontal cortex—located directly behind our forehead—which allows us the opportunity to choose whether to react or respond.

Watching the grizzly on the other side of the river, knowing it could reach us in minutes, prevented my mind from thinking about anything not related to my survival.

You are noticing the pattern, right? When we find ourselves in heightened states of awareness, the internal board meeting is suspended and the nine personalities in the room move into solution mode. Together, they will determine if we will respond or react to an unanticipated situation. Your primary dialogues will be your commanders whenever you feel threatened.

So, you may want to consider whether your primary dialogues support the best version of you—your ideal state.

Our Most Valuable Currency

How we spend our time reveals our primary dialogues and determines how we identify ourselves. What you spend time **doing** inspires how you spend time **thinking**, which, in turn, determines how you *feel*.

Change is a requirement of progress, and change always comes at a cost. If we are interested in enriching our experience of life, we must be willing to make adjustments when the *quality of behaviour* we are engaged with does not support our ideal state. One of the most profound adjustments we can make is in relation to how we spend our time. This is, often, the point where Self-realization comes into conflict with secondary gain.

"Secondary gain is defined as the advantage that occurs secondary to stated or real illness." [051]

You may want to lose weight, but you would miss the sympathy people give you because of your "struggle."

You may want out of your "going nowhere" relationship, but are afraid to be alone, without the validation, sex, and predictability of a relationship.

You may be dissatisfied with your job and want to move on, although you receive tremendous social validation through your workplace. You may feel insecure about your ability to earn respect within an alternate work environment, in which you would be far from an expert on anything.

Secondary gain is always present in a situation where people say one thing and do another. Uncovering secondary gain often casts a spotlight on the *zero point*, or **source point**, of any habitual behaviour or neurosis.

A source point can be understood as any of the *qualities of behaviour* represented within the archetypes/*I Ching*.

The Psychology of Time

Psychologist and Stanford Professor Emeritus, Phil Zimbardo, defines **Time Perspective** as "the study of how individuals divide the flow of human experience into different time frames or time zones—automatically and non-consciously."

In his book, *The Time Perspective*, he explains that each time tense (past, present, and future) has two perspectives, creating six specific categories for relating to our experience of time: Past *Positive*, Past *Negative*, Present *Hedonism (enjoying life)* or Present *Fatalism (fate is determined)*, Future: *Life/Goal-Oriented* or Future *Transcendental/Death is the Beginning.*

When we begin to consider the way we perceive our experience of time, we become aware of our predispositions. Awareness always allows us a greater opportunity to adjust belief systems that are not oriented towards maintaining our ideal state.

Zimbardo also suggests how to achieve an Optimal State. What do you think? What combination of Time Tense categories do you feel would support your ideal state?

"Success is an effect, not a cause. If we want to secure the effect, we must ascertain the cause, idea, or thought by which the effect is created." [#008]

~ Charles Haanel

Challenge 2: The Currency of Time

Purpose: To identify if there is a dichotomy between how I spend my time in support of my ideal state. At any time, I may replace any of my primary dialogues. As such, I must be willing to make adjustments to how I invest time. This challenge will build an awareness of how I spend my time as a reflection of what I value.

Tools: Notebook, Pencil, Audio Recorder

Instructions: Begin by reviewing the last few days. In your notebook, determine how much time you spent doing specific daily activities. Do this in the same manner as though you were budgeting financially. When you have completed this, extend the budgeted time from the last few days to the last few weeks. Notice what similarities exist. What have you been doing with your time, consistently, over the last few weeks? What takes up large percentages of your time? Social life? Work? Reading? Practising the tuba? Hula hooping? Family?

Report your findings into your audio recorder.

*Give yourself extra credit for;

1) Identifying primary dialogues that do not support your desired ideal state.

2) Uncovering the secondary gain that has kept you invested in these unsupportive behaviours.

~3~

Looking across the river at the large grizzly as the sun rapidly set, I remember thinking my life was in danger. I called over my fellow hiker. We assessed the situation and came up with some options:

1) We could take our tent down and move further up the glacier, which would present its own danger, as the sun was rapidly going down.

2) We could take our tent down and start hiking back towards the road, although we would soon be hiking in the dark within our furry friend's established territory.

3) We could stay exactly where we were.

Sometimes doing nothing is the hardest because this works against our solution-oriented mind. I resigned myself to the advice of Marko, my more experienced hiking companion.

Indo-European

The common symbols represented throughout comparative mythology and religions are referred to as **Elementary Ideas.**

New concepts and ideas develop by similar methods as evolution, by adding to an existing structure.

Our major and historical holidays have evolved from pagan festivals, and even the days of the week still honour the polytheistic worldview of those who came before us.

The origin of the Norse worldview originated from Indo-European and Germanic folklore. While a comparative study is not our current topic, it is wise to keep in mind that the pantheistic worldview of the classical period of mythology—which has largely been forgotten and discarded—originated within a matriarchal Vanir consciousness, as experienced by nomadic hunter-gatherers.

NORSE	ROMAN	MODERN
SUN-DAY	SUN	SUNDAY
MOON-DAY	MOON	MONDAY
TIW'S DAY	MARS	TUESDAY
WOTEN'S DAY	MERCURY	WEDNESDAY
THOR'S DAY	JUPITER	THURSDAY
FREYJA'S DAY	VENUS	FRIDAY
SATURN'S DAY	SATURN	SATURDAY

The development of mathematics and written language allowed the "high" civilizations of Mesopotamia, Greece, Asia, the Indus Valley, and South America to begin mapping out the cosmos, and gave rise to the concept of gods (polytheism) who resided beyond the earth, ruled by an "all father" who was destined to become the solitary god of monotheism.

Evidence of Homo sapiens on Orkney Island (Northern Scotland) in the "ceramic Mesolithic" Period (circa 7000 BCE), and established settlements by the Neolithic Period (4000 BCE), provide a surreal context to the extent of Homo sapiens exodus from East Africa. The Ring of Brodgar is a Neolithic stone circle (henge) that is estimated to have been erected between 2500-2000 BCE. This was during the golden age of Ur, in Mesopotamia, the Indus Valley Civilization in India, the Fifth Dynasty of Egypt, the Lagash Dynasty of Sumer.

In the *Prose Edda*, [052] Gangleri (the name used by the first recorded King in Scandinavia when he was in disguise) has a conversation with Óðinn about the origin of all things. He is told that Múspellsheimr was the first world to exist, and after "many ages," Niflheimr was created.

As part of the truce between the Vanir (old pantheon) and the Æsir (new), Njord [053] and his son Frey were sent to live among the Æsir. Joining them was Frey's twin sister, Freyja.

VANIR	AESIR	CELESTIAL	GREEK	CHRISTIAN	PSYCHE	MALE	FEMALE
NJORD	ODINN	NEPTUNE	ZEUS	FATHER	SELF		
FREYR	TYR	MARS	HERMES	JESUS	ANIMUS	EGO	
FREYJA	FRIGG	VENUS	APHRODITE	HOLY SPIRIT	ANIMA		EGO

Psyche may be defined as the human soul, mind, or spirit, [054]—the totality of elements forming the mind. [055] In Jungian terms, Anima//Animus, ego and Self.

"We borrowed the word psyche directly from Greek into English. In Greek mythology, Psyche was a beautiful princess who fell in love with Eros (Cupid), god of love, and went through terrible trials before being allowed to marry him. The story is often understood to be about the soul redeeming itself through love. (To the Greeks, psyche also meant 'butterfly,' which suggests how they imagined the soul.) In English, psyche often sounds less spiritual than soul, less intellectual than mind, and more private than personality." [056]

The Opiate Function

Fear and anxiety produce a kind of opiate function, which inhibits our ability to discern if a response or a reaction is more appropriate. This distinction cannot be overstated. If a loved one were just out of surgery, would you prefer to hear that they are responding to the surgery? Or reacting to it?

If the mind is consumed with thoughts of snakes filling us with venom, or how it would feel to be torn apart by a frenzied grizzly bear, then we may not have the mental faculty to respond appropriately to the conditions we are facing because our thoughts have prematurely projected us into an anxiety/fear state, which may trigger an instinctive impulse.

Let me take this opportunity to mention, again, that your nine primary dialogues will be the commanders of your internal resources when you feel threatened. You should probably keep this thought at the forefront of your mind.

All right, so are you still tapping your foot? If you stopped, when did you stop? What new thought hijacked your attention? Identify this as you begin tapping the opposite foot.

Meanwhile, Back in the Yukon . . .

The advice of Marco, the more experienced hiker, was to remain where we were. Perhaps because hiding in plain sight would be a discouragement to a bear, who may prefer the tactical advantage of trees to launch an attack and quickly escape if something were to go wrong. It is just as likely that Marco was speaking with such confidence because he could sense my trepidation and wanted to replace my anxiety with peace. Regardless, I didn't sleep at all. Every crack of the ice, which is constant on a glacier, was the sound of a rabid grizzly bear anticipating his next massacre. Marco, on the other hand, was asleep within minutes, which only added to my anxiety. I felt it necessary to stay alert—as if it would make much difference—should the grizzly come at us.

This paralyzing effect of thought is **strong** enough to keep us terrified of imaginary situations we are helpless to change, and **bold** enough to inspire one to defend themselves against an attacking, non-venomous stick.

Alternatively, we may utilize our thoughts as a powerful tool when we begin to imagine our ideal state. When thought is directed towards a specific feeling that supports our ideal future, we stimulate confidence and crush insecurity.

To generate the momentum required to form a clear picture of your ideal state *with the intention of manifesting your ideal future*, you may begin by replacing unsupportive dialogues with supportive ones.

I invite you to *feel* your ideal state. Imagine it until you *feel* it.

As we begin to identify our primary dialogues, we may discover that the "voices" we have come to think of as "our own" have their origin in belief systems inherited by others. Perhaps, while useful in the past, they are no longer relevant to our ideal future.

We identify our primary dialogues so that we may adjust those that are unsupportive of our ideal state. This is our response-ability. An unwillingness to take this incentive is an intentional sabotage of our potential for inner peace.

Fostering Recognition

Recognition may be understood as awareness. Awareness may be understood as consciousness. Thus, if we want to facilitate Individuation—making the unconscious conscious—then we must take the initiative to recognize our habitual thoughts and behaviour. The more regularly we do so, the more we will cultivate a habit of Self-examination.

Imagine you are a wildlife biologist and you have just started a new job studying the animal of your choice. As part of your research, you will collect information about feeding and mating times, conditions that cause agitation, etc.

If you go into the field for just one day and write your report, how will your data compare to another biologist who spent every day for the last three years in the field? Whose results do you think will be more reliable and credible?

In our journey to know ourselves, we must consider ourselves *full time observers of our own behaviour.* This means we are constantly "in the field," making notes regarding what influences and impacts the choices we make, the emotions we express, and the thoughts that inspire behaviour.

Mindfulness refines the skills of observation required for this task. You may also consider starting a regular journal. Better yet, an audio journal. When you speak out loud, it is easier to remain concentrated on your object of thought. When you hear yourself speak, perspective is challenged without defenses or an *expectation of sympathy* that may arise if you were speaking to another. Words become affirmations, and confidence becomes form.

Challenge 3: 8-Point Index

Purpose: I will examine the lessons I have learned in the last week.

Tools: Audio recorder, notebook, pen

Instructions: Start by reviewing the last seven days. What are some things you have learned about yourself and others? You may not assume these are significant, but list them anyway. Perhaps you learned that your cat prefers dry food, or that you sleep better on your back than on your left side. The more information you can come up with, the better. Next, create categories such as "others," "me," and "work" as a way of organizing these lessons into distinct categories.

When you have gone through this process, create an 8-point index, by which you can summarize how you've changed during the last seven days.

Next, repeat this process, looking beyond the week. Allow yourself to examine how you have changed within the current season you are in (fall, winter, etc.).

* Give yourself bonus points for repeating this process while examining a previous season.

** The effects of this challenge will be exponential if you speak out loud into your audio recorder.

~4~

All right, so you've still got your toe tapping? Great. Now begin alternating between your left and right foot.

The way to master your destiny and be the creator of your ideal state, *now*, is to ensure your predominant mental attitude supports your ideal state. We do not have to find ourselves in a life-threatening situation to maintain a heightened state of awareness. We can begin by exploring the *qualities of behaviour* that our primary dialogues inspire. If these dialogues are not supportive of your ideal state, the good news is that you can replace them with new dialogues. This may take some work, and I can tell you that this investment will multiply exponentially.

A heightened state of awareness is facilitated through mindfulness, and I invite you to replace unsupportive dialogues with things you are absolutely in control of, like breath and posture. These two primary dialogues are so great because they remind us that we are in complete control of how we *feel*. There are two distinct forms of using breath to cultivate awareness; one for each brain hemisphere.

We may refer to the first method as **conscious breathing**, which may be inhaling to a four count and exhaling to a four count. This is something that can be done throughout the day to support a calm and empowering mental attitude, and the best part is, no one can prevent you from taking this step towards awareness. Remind yourself, constantly, to breathe this way to calm down, and eventually, this conscious behaviour will be taken up by the subconscious, creating room for *a new intentional conscious primary dialogue.*

All subconscious behaviour originated as conscious choice.

The second type of breathing we may refer to as **unconscious breath awareness**, and it is *just as essential* to maintaining harmony of the psyche. In this scenario, we sit quietly for a designated duration of time without trying to control the breath—just observe it.

Huginn and Muninn

Huginn and Muninn are Óðinn's ravens. Each day they are sent into the nine worlds to gather information about what is happening and report back to Óðinn.

Huginn is derived from húg or hugr (thought). Muninn is derived from munr, which is often translated as desire, though embodies broader *qualities of behaviour*, such as passion, enthusiasm, plans and ambitions, wishes and hopes. Muninn is also related to the root minni (memory)—a more passive quality than, say, enthusiasm, which is present and future tense–and lends itself to past-tense mindset.

"The two names therefore can't be neatly distinguished from one another; they overlap to the point of being virtually synonymous." [058]

"Huginn and Muninn don't have distinct personalities. They're a duplicate form of the same underlying idea. More specifically, their names refer to their being concrete visualized forms of the 'thought' of Óðinn.

In the Norse worldview, the Self is comprised of numerous different parts that are semi-autonomous and can detach from one another under certain circumstances. These detached parts are frequently imagined in an animal form that corresponds to their underlying character.

In the case of Huginn and Muninn, they're Óðinn's intellectual/ spiritual capabilities journeying outward in the form of fittingly intelligent and curious birds that also resonate with Óðinn's roles as a battle god and death god." [059]

~ Daniel McCoy

The cyclical nature of thought/will and desire/enthusiasm, is such that change can be integrated when we focus, with intention, on replacing the *quality of behaviour* of either. By replacing unsupportive thoughts with ones that support our ideal state, we discover a fountain of desire, motivation, enthusiasm, and the resource of memory. In addition to his pair of ravens, Huginn and Muninn, Óðinn also has a pair of wolves, Geri and Freki. Both names can be translated "the ravenous" or "the greedy one," and we may understand these wolves to be the shadow of thought/will and desire/enthusiasm.

"Galdor is the art and practice of first hearing, then understanding the runic words of the ravens, and finally, putting their words to work in the world. The ravens are, of course, mythic codes for certain parts of the soul or psyche." [021] ~ Edred Thorsson

Sleep and Hydration

Take a moment and imagine the last time you were tired. Now imagine a time when you were exaggeratingly tired. Were you at your best in this state? What impact does a tired state have on your ability to make decisions? Are you more prone to respond or react to unanticipated situations? How would others say you behave when you are short of sleep?

We will likely all agree that being excessively tired is not an ideal state. What do we tend to do when we find ourselves feeling tired and groggy? Many of us consume stimulants that deceive our brain into believing our body is not fatigued, and thus, overwhelm the body with increased activity.

Between stimulants and the increased activity, we fail to recognize that a lack of sleep is the *source point* of our daily frustrations. With an increased inability to identify the source point of our *feeling*, we tend to misdirect our frustration towards others, as though external sources must be to blame for how we identify ourselves.

When the body is tired or dehydrated, we become sluggish and fatigued. We are less prone to respond and more likely to react. Our cerebral cortex—the willpower machine of our brain—begins to look like the dried-up avocado that you have been holding in your imagination. When muscles are not used, they begin to entropy. We start mistaking twigs for rattlesnakes and cracking ice for grizzly bear footsteps.

Masaru Emoto was a modern pioneer in the correlation between water and consciousness.

"Emoto believed that water was a 'blueprint for our reality' and that emotional 'energies' and 'vibrations' could change the physical structure of water. Emoto's water crystal experiments consisted of exposing water in glasses to different words, pictures, or music, and then freezing and examining the aesthetic properties of the resulting crystals with microscopic photography. Emoto made the claim that water exposed to positive speech and thoughts would result in visually 'pleasing' crystals being formed when that water was frozen, and that negative intention would yield 'ugly' frozen crystal formations." [#060]

Óðinn sacrificed an eye for a drink of water, which contains cosmic knowledge. Perhaps it's time we began to recognize how "cosmic knowledge" and hydration may be either sides of the same coin.

Meanwhile, Back in the Desert . . .

As it turns out, we were never more than two hundred yards from our van the entire afternoon. In our minds, we were "lost" once we suggested it to ourselves, and the mind confirmed this experience by blinding our attention to anything that would have prevented us from "seeing" the experience we desired. We "desired" the experience because we chose to think about it.

The more attention I give a thought or idea, the more it becomes the cause that will produce a corresponding effect, regardless of demonstrable truth.

We *thought* we were lost because we didn't know where we were, although we were not as lost as we feared. Unsure of which direction would lead to our van, each of us walked in a different direction without ever losing eye contact with the person closest to us.

Thirty minutes later, we were drowning ourselves in the reserves of water at a nearby gas station, laughing off the whole experience while simultaneously relieved that our imagination could only alter our perception and *not, yet*, manifest our greatest fears.

It is vital to not underestimate the value of others. Interaction with others is essential perspective and may also provide accountability and honesty, which are helpful on our journey.

The journey towards Ragnarök—Individuation—is facilitated by the people and conditions we experience throughout our lifetime. Each person is a symbolic projection and a reflection of our personal illusions, engineered to "awaken" us to our repressed/denied potential before we wander too far away from our ideal state and become "lost" in the desert (timestreams) of our internal dialogues.

There are sixty-four timestreams; each may be identified with a *quality of behaviour* as represented in the *I Ching*.

In his book, *Mindfulness Integrated CBT for Well-Being and Personal Growth*, Bruno Cayoun identifies what he refers to as the *Co-emergence Model of Reinforcement* in equilibrium state. It goes like this; **Situation** leads to **Sensory Perception,** leads to **Evaluation,** leads to **Introspection,** leads to **Reaction or Chosen Response,** leads back to **Sensory Perception** . . . and the cycle continues to repeat itself until a new, greater situation arises, and a new cycle begins.

When introspection—or any stage—is diminished, Cayoun refers to this as "*System in Disequilibrium,*" which "increases our tendency to rely on knowledge and assumptions stored in memory and react rapidly." [#046]

"To better explain how this applies to our mind, the co-emergence model of reinforcement combines Western psychological understanding of emotions with the so-called 'five aggregates' of the mind in Buddhist psychology to describe how our mind works when we learn to respond in a certain way." [046]

~ Dr. Bruno A. Cayoun

A Fourfold Personality

"Everywhere in myths and religious symbolism there appears the model of the fourfold structure of the psyche." [014]

~ Marie-Louise Von Franz

Imagine a circle with a giant addition symbol dividing it like a pie cut into four pieces. Now, focus on the addition sign. At the top of the vertical line, *in your mind's eye*, write "thinking." At the bottom of the vertical line, write "feeling." To the left of the horizontal line, write "intuition," and to the right, "sensation."

Together, these two poles of psyche—rational/evaluative and irrational/perceptual—form the axis upon which our destiny is woven.

"Where, under optimum conditions, three functions become conscious, this has the effect of also changing the basic structure of the psyche. Neither in psychology nor in any other field of reality is there ever a one-sided course of action, for if the unconscious builds up a field of consciousness, the repercussion of such a change produces an alteration in the unconscious structure as well . . . due to the counteraction, even the basic structure of the psyche has a changed or modified form." [014]

~ Marie-Louise Von Franz

Do you rely on thinking more than feeling? Do you rely on sensation rather than intuition?

Challenge 4: Uncover Your Fourfold Personality

Purpose: To identify the superior and inferior functions of your personality.

Tools: Notebook, pen, audio recorder

Instructions: Draw on paper the diagram you hold in your mind (+). Speaking aloud, consider each of the following types: Thinking and Feeling (evaluative, motive pole), and Intuition and Sensation (perceptual, emotive pole). Which one of these four qualities of behaviour best represents you? Do not ask yourself what type you would like to be, but which most often determines your action. The most habitual behaviour is your superior function. The quality opposite your superior function (of the same pole) is your inferior function.

Place your superior function at the top of the vertical pole. At the bottom of the vertical line, write the other word that corresponds to the same pole (inferior function). The horizontal line will represent the second pole, creating the configuration of your fourfold personality. You may have a dominant quality represented in your horizontal pole that supports your superior function.

*Bonus points for determining whether you are an introvert or an extrovert. Again, do not choose what you would like to be, but which typically represents how you spend time?

Recommended Reading:

Lecture on Jung's Typology, Marie von Franz and James Hillman

~5~

Living Mythos came as a result of mapping out constellations of experience as though I were recording celestial movements.

Habits and tendencies were examined and scrutinized in an effort to understand how my choices were contributing to cyclical patterns and conditions. I felt as though I were running on a proverbial wheel without the ability to anticipate transitions, and I eagerly sought to discover a way to stop this, or at least slow it down.

Individuation creates the illusion of time slowing down because– in the moments between inhale and exhale–we may begin to observe patterns of habitual behaviour, which are the "cause" of conditions in our life. We may then adjust our behaviour and influence the "effect."

Our choice to react or respond is the "cause," and conditions produced by our choice is the "effect."

Intention is thought concentrated on *motive*, which can produce an incredible amount of creative energy when supported by desire and enthusiasm.

Arriving at this **point of intention** is the subject of my first book, *Regressions*, in which unconscious patterns of belief are brought into conscious experience. This process leads one to re-evaluate whether existing *qualities of behaviour* are supporting our desired ideal state.

Gangleri

Throughout Norse mythology, the characters we encounter frequently have multiple names. As we have previously mentioned, the Swedish King,

Gylfi, while wandering in disguise, used the alternate name Gangleri. "Gangleri" became synonymous with "wandering," and Óðinn was referred to by this name to establish context for a specific story.

It may be understood that the *quality of behaviour* of characters within a story, implies who they are. If I were telling you a story about Gangleri, as he was wandering through the nine worlds, it would not be necessary for me tell you I was referring to Óðinn because it would be obvious that a Swedish King could not travel through the nine worlds. You would already understand the context (Óðinn the wanderer, in disguise), and I could move straight to the point. Additionally, these stories may intentionally have been more ambiguous than we are accustomed to, for the sake of being as widely relatable as possible. It is not so much about the characters, as it is about how the story will affect the *quality of behaviour* of the listener.

To give you some further perspective, Óðinn has over two hundred names. [061] Each name contains specific *qualities of behaviour* associated with his personality.

When King Gangleri is speaking with the **Óðinnic Triad** in the *Prose Edda*, the Triad is referred to as High, Just-as-High, and Third—each a pseudonym for Óðinn. [062] It is just as likely that Vili and Vé, Óðinn's two brothers, are also indicative of Óðinn's triune personality. This concept will have become familiar to us, now, as ego, Self, and Anima//Animus. Given this revelation, Freyja's "infidelity" is exposed as a metaphor for the Triad aspects of Óðinn.

Mythology, in its most literal sense, is primitive psychology; echoes from a time when we had not yet developed the cognitive ability to express psyche from a Self-realized, fourth perceptual position.

Achievable Goals

Six months after *Regressions* was released, I found myself confronting the darkness of my illusions. It seemed as though the process of writing *Regressions* had awakened a sleeping giant, upon who's body the Individuation process would ravage.

Unconscious belief systems took form within the great chasm that had been created, separating my illusions from "reality." An awareness of emerging belief systems from the unconscious prompted me to begin pattern tracking, and four years later, *Living Mythos* is the result.

From the "yawning void" of that creative potential, I have emerged a completely different person.

We may begin by identifying stories we tell ourselves by considering how the choices we make today are based on the belief systems of yesterday. Do yesterday's belief systems support your ideal state of tomorrow?

We often engage in behaviour that is unsupportive of our ideal state. Recognition of this brings the unconscious into conscious awareness. With this new awareness, we become empowered to make different choices, just as a massage may make you aware of tension you had been storing in your muscles.

Pattern tracking begins as an effort to identify unconscious habitual behaviour. It becomes an adventure when you realize pattern tracking creates the potential for empowerment, and, subsequently, transformation. At the same time that I began pattern tracking, I made the decision to quit smoking. I call this **stacking change**, which is, essentially, pairing up a change in *thought* with a change in *behaviour*.

We only have a given amount of willpower reserve, so we are more interested in cultivating a practice of moderation than of enforcing absolutes.

Moderation is predicated upon maintaining our ideal state. This demands integrity and honesty between the functions of our triune brain.

Once we begin to know how moderation works, and our priorities reflect and support our ideal state, our behaviour will reinforce our conviction. Unsupportive habits will dissolve effortlessly.

Intention is everything. When we are motivated to change by terms like "good" and "bad" (monotheism), we simply repress our desire and neglect the opportunity to discover the *source point* for the craving or revulsion, which is prompting our habitual behaviour. By repressing this, it will find an alternate method to project itself into the objective world until we bring the unconscious source point into conscious awareness and transcend the neurosis.

Awareness of the cause is usually enough to eliminate the effect. By reverse-engineering this process, we discover that the same principle applies to attracting desirable effects.

I quit smoking when I desired smoking most of all—in the midst of confronting my personal great illusions. From within the timestreams, I reasoned that if I could quit smoking when my desire was great, then it would be easy to not smoke after my desire had faded.

This worked because I substituted my desire to smoke with a desire to not smell like cigarettes during a two-month yoga challenge.

I had never done yoga before, I just needed something to distract me from getting lost in my Self-directed condemnation.

I quit smoking a day at a time. I set daily goals to not smoke THAT DAY and achieved a big-picture goal by focusing on my daily accomplishments. This strategy allows one to measure accomplishment and restores confidence in our ability to create sustainable change in our life. Starting small, with achievable goals, is an important step in reclaiming our outsourced willpower.

When the "genius" ego mind hears, "I will never smoke again, ever," it reacts the way you would expect. It **craves** what it cannot have, which stimulates **aversion** towards our perceived weakness.

Craving and aversion are identified as the source of all suffering in Buddhist philosophy.

When you feel empowered, life is not a series of events that just happen; rather, experience unfolds organically. We become a participant in our destiny, instead of a bystander/victim. Life is happening *for* us, not *to* us.

This concept is supported by the role of the Three Norns of Norse mythology, who weave a fluid destiny for man, in contrast to the three fates of Greek mythology whose "fates" are considered absolute.

We become so overwhelmed by what we cannot change that we neglect the things we can.

Authentic Relationships

Once choice becomes habitual, we lose the ability to objectively discern how it is affecting us. Try removing a regular part of your diet, like sugar or caffeine, for two weeks. When you reintroduce this to your diet, you will bring the unconscious effects of your consumption into conscious awareness. This *knowledge allows us to adjust our behaviour.*

We must reclaim our power and take response-ability for the conditions we invite into our life by acknowledging how we contribute to the conditions we encounter.

This same principle applies to all of our relationships. We become the five people we spend the most time with. We are what we eat. Same principle.

You may begin by paying attention to how you *feel* before, during, and after spending time with others.

The first *quality of behaviour* I look for in others is their eagerness to actually **listen**. If they don't, or if they listen only for an opportunity to speak, then I am not really interested in pursuing a relationship.

The second *quality of behaviour* that is essential to authentic relationship is **non-judgement**.

My friend Les is a consistent and inspirational example of this. Our friendship illustrates the **non-judgement clause**, which is a mutual agreement to not judge one another. This opens the way for **honesty**. When Les offers his perspective, he is not undermining my ability to make a decision. He also knows that I understand this, so he does not hesitate to be honest and offer his authentic perspective. Because I trust his intent, I don't feel defensive if his perspective is different than mine. I **listen without trying to defend** myself because an opinion that is different from mine does not threaten me. A different opinion is not a judgement against me. Rather, I anticipate expanding and enhancing my perspective by listening.

It's as though we are at the ice cream shop shouting out flavours as we notice them, with no implication that the flavours we see are any more appealing than the flavours the other can see.

Mutual Agreements

One brisk January morning, with a fresh blanket of snow as our canvas, I enthusiastically shared with Les my theory/discovery of the dualistic nature of communication; **solution** oriented and **sympathy** oriented. As our conversation proceeded, Les mentioned how important it must be, then, for us to not judge solution-oriented communicators for not offering us sympathy. This seems obvious, now, but at the time, I realized I was holding an incredible amount of people up to standards of behaviour that were not in their nature.

Expectations inevitably lead to disappointment, especially when the expectations are unrealistic. Disappointment leads to resentment, because it reminds us of our capacity to manipulate others.

The "non-judgement clause" is a necessary tool that is of service as we continue our journey towards the inevitable fate of the gods, Ragnarök.

Accountability and integrity are the offspring of non-judgement.

It is important to reinforce the right to disagree.

Persona

Persona has been defined as, *"the aspect of someone's character that is presented to, or perceived by others."* [063]

The word is derived from Latin, *"where it originally referred to a theatrical mask. Its meaning in the latter Roman period changed to indicate a 'character' of a theatrical performance or court of law, when it became apparent that different individuals could assume the same role."* [065]

In Jungian psychology, persona is *"the mask or facade presented to satisfy the demands of the situation or the environment, and not representing the inner personality of the individual."* [066]

Regardless of which persona we are wearing, ego attempts to relate the human experience to Self.

Authentic personas may facilitate contained relationships where it may not be ecological to be our authentic Self. For example, a work persona facilitates functioning in the subtle social environment of workplace conditions where it may not be appropriate or advised to get too personal. We may also have a domestic persona, suitable for maintaining relationships with family and extended family. These personas may be separate from our "friend" and "acquaintance" personas, which may be slightly (or extremely) different versions of one another.

We may, also, have a legion of false personas. False personas are a contradiction to authenticity, typical of fantasy/illusion, in which we attempt to convince others (and ourselves) that we are the personification of our great illusion.

False personas influence our decisions. We may not, logically, believe our lies/illusions, but the subconscious mind does not discriminate or make value judgements. Eventually our illusions will be taken up by the subconscious and form inherent beliefs about our "reality."

It is the function of the conscious mind that differentiates dreams from our waking state, and illusions from authenticity.

We make decisions based on the subtle *feeling* that our stories inspire. All co-dependent relationships are a relationship between false personas.

Challenge 5: Identify Personas

Purpose: I will recognize my personas as distinct from Self.

Tools: Notebook, pen, audio recorder

Instructions: Identify as many distinct personas as you can, ensuring a minimum of five. For each persona, ask yourself;

1) What part of me, what dynamic in my inner life, does this persona represent?

2) What benefit does this persona provide?

3) How does this persona conceal my authenticity?

~6~

At this point, you have probably figured out that I consider honesty a personal response-ability. Any gesture towards transformation and Self-knowledge is contingent upon specific and targeted honesty on your part, because unless we critically examine all of our belief systems and assumptions about "reality" and eagerly eliminate unsupportive dialogues, we will never reach the fullness of our potential—a potential that transcends anything we have previously imagined.

A general understanding of how personal experience is extracted from collective/universal *qualities of behaviour* reminds us of the subjective nature of individual reality. This explains why two children raised in the same house can grow up to be so different.

How we cope with our unique experience shapes our personality, while the collective experiences we share (archetypal templates) provide the context by which our relationships take form.

Fenrir

The wolf, Fenrir, migrated from Indo-European folklore into Norse mythology, where he is presented as the son of Loki, and father of Hati (hatred) and Sköll (mockery), the two wolves who chase the Sun and Moon, and will catch them during the final battle of Ragnarök. Fenrir is the brother of *Jörmungandr*—a great serpent large enough to encircle all of Midgard—and his sister is the underworld goddess, Hel.

Aware of his potential for destruction, the gods kidnap Fenrir and keep him prisoner in Asgard. Fenrir grows in strength and ferocity, so it is decided by the gods that Fenrir should be bound. However, Fenrir easily breaks free of the bindings. They try again, convincing Fenrir that this is a game. Again, he breaks loose. Finally, the gods enlist the help of the Dwarves, who forge the strongest chain ever.

By this time, Fenrir has some doubts about the gods' intentions. He agrees to be bound, only if one of the gods will place a hand in his mouth. Týr is the only god who volunteers, knowing full well what will happen when Fenrir discovers he has been tricked into prolonged captivity.

Sure enough, once Fenrir is bound with the chain, he bites down and Týr sacrifices his hand.

Fenrir is synonymous with Freki, one of Óðinn's wolves, who represents the shadow of Huginn (thought/will) and Muninn (desire/enthusiasm), in the *Poetic Edda* poem, *Völuspá*.

Considering Fenrir will swallow Óðinn at Ragnarök, this is quite revealing. It's as though death is foreshadowed, only by an ambition to create.

"Óðinn feeds one Freki at his dinner table and another—Fenrir—with his flesh during the events of Ragnarök." [067]

~ John Lindow

Anchoring the Ideal State

Natural laws provide the foundation upon which we successfully build our ideal future and anchor our ideal state. The law of growth states that the individual is complete at all times, and this makes it possible to receive only as we give.

"We give thought. We receive thought, which is substance in equilibrium and is constantly being differentiated in form by what we think." [008]

~ Charles Haanel

If we want to facilitate authentic communication and relationships, we must take **response**-ability for our thoughts, time, and money—all of which are outlets whereby we channel energy to be transmuted into form (alchemy).

Giving of our time, money, etc., is an energetic investment and is manifested by where our creative energy is channeled—hence, what you spend time doing and thinking will reveal itself in the conditions of your life.

This experience is pleasant if our subconscious decisions are in harmony with our ideal state.

Cultivating a Habit of Listening

Becoming aware of unconscious belief systems may also bring to our attention belief systems that are working *for* us.

One of the greatest and most profound habits I learned as a child was the power of listening. Making friends and gaining favour with others is easy if you **listen** to people.

If you actually listen to what people say, not for the opportunity to redirect the conversation back to your experiences, but if you **listen to reframe**, you will not only allow others to feel heard, you become aware of the archetypal template that is rising up from the unconscious.

Our interactions with others and the feelings we have towards them, for good or ill, provide us with invaluable insight into unconscious archetypes we may not be acknowledging—ones trying to make their presence become more significant in our life.

Denying these reflections causes us to regress and repress, which perpetuates assumption and illusion.

When you *listen to reframe*, walls are broken down, and you discover that everyone you speak with will become an open reference book of experiences you may learn from. These interactions allow us to observe the experience without being possessed by it.

Listening facilitates non-judgement, and when people do not feel judged, they will tell you almost anything.

By the time I was in high school, the phrases "I can't believe I am telling you this," or "I've never told anyone this before," were phrases I heard from others on a regular basis. Cultivating this *quality of behaviour* has remained an incredible asset.

> *"The true method of concentration is to become so identified with your object of thought that you're conscious of nothing else."* [008]
>
> ~ Charles Haanel

It is important to develop our ability to listen effectively. I invite you to consider listening as an activity that may be enhanced by single-minded concentration.

The true method of **listening** is to become so interested in what another is saying that you are thinking of nothing else.

The true method of **empathy** is to become so identified with what another is feeling that you are conscious of nothing else. The shadow of empathy is possession.

The true method of **compassion** is to become so identified with what another is experiencing that you are compelled to do something to ease their suffering.

Meanwhile, Back in the Yukon . . .

After a long night of imagining horrific ways a grizzly could end my life, the sun came up. It never felt so good to be alive!

Through the night, I had composed a mental list of things I would do differently, and things I would never do again.

We made breakfast, packed up our cocoon tent, and made our way back towards the road.

As we arrived back at the highway, Marco, my fellow hiker, casually mentioned that he had recently finished a book detailing some of the most gruesome grizzly attacks.

I thanked him for not sharing the contents, as my imagination had done a good enough job of tormenting me. I silently wondered how he had been able to sleep so peacefully.

It is not required that we face our own mortality to instigate change, though it often turns out this way. Funerals are a common catalyst for introspection. We do not have to wait for funerals and life-threatening situations, though. Introspection is always a factor in the process of thought, regardless of whether we are conscious of its role or not.

Introspection may play a diminished role in this process when we are settled into routine.

Fostering an Ideal State

Wandering minds, frequently caught up in memories of the past or possibilities of the future, make concentration impossible, and mastery an impossibility. Cultivating mindfulness nurtures our ability to authentically listen to others and promotes well-being, honesty, and personal **response-**ability. These are *qualities of behaviour* that will enrich our life and the lives of those we interact with.

The ability to direct attention (which includes time, money, and other available resources) on a desired condition is the method by which we support our ideal state.

Natural law requires a harmonious relationship between ego, Self, and Anima//Animus. Most people default to a monotheistic philosophy to govern the mind. As we will discover, this is not the only option available.

Our power to manifest conditions is predicated on *action with intention*. This process originates within us and flows forth into the objective when we take the initiative to adjust our behaviour to support our ideal state.

Monotheism breaks down when we direct our attention towards personal response-ability.

When ego comes into harmony with our motive (will/thought) and emotive (desire/enthusiasm) poles—Huginn and Muninn, respectively—the emergence of a fourth perceptual position begins to manifest, as represented by Óðinn the wanderer; Óðinn the *conscious* observer, observing.

Vacation State

Vacations are so enjoyable because we create an opportunity to leave behind our "regular world" anxieties, concerns, and stresses that we have come to accept as normal conditions of experience.

While on vacation, we become curious about our new surroundings and experience an intentional **pattern interrupt** that allows us to enter a heightened state of awareness while relaxed.

By intentionally creating a vacation state, we can anchor ourselves to the curiosity that accompanies a predominant mental attitude that suggests life is unfolding *for* us, instead of *to* us.

Curiosity trumps contempt. A vacation state is a perfect transition into a fully-realized ideal state because it allows us to enter a heightened state of awareness, without the experience of fear.

Challenge 6: Vacation State

Purpose: To liberate myself from past judgements and conditioning.

Tools: Audio Recorder

Instructions: How do you imagine others see you when you are not in a relaxed state? How different is your behaviour when you are on vacation? While speaking into your audio recorder, recall three to five times when you felt completely free of obligations. As you recall these instances, see yourself. Become an observer and imagine how you may have looked to others, in your relaxed state.

Next, go outside—perhaps for a walk or to the grocery store—and do your best to maintain the feeling of relaxation that you enjoyed in the memories you recalled earlier. Feel free to visualize your vacation as you are doing your grocery shopping; hum a tune you heard while on vacation. You may even want to dig out some article of clothing that you wore while on your vacation to help anchor this vacation state to your present experience.

-7-

Experience flows out from specific archetypal templates we refer to as *qualities of behaviour*. They are reliable because they are causes that consistently produce a definite measurable effect—the conditions we encounter in life.

These *qualities of behaviour* are compatible with natural law, and we may anticipate the effect of our thoughts, with an understanding that thought determines perspective and perspective changes *our* experience. We may become navigators of our experience. We are never the pilot. The "pilot" is the unfolding process. Free will only influences the "version" of the process we experience.

By facilitating a harmonious relationship between desires, dreams, and destiny—Anima/Self, ego, and Self/Animus—we may achieve inner peace and become masters of our experience.

Healthy relationships possess a specific *quality of behaviour* that allow for the expression of perspective without feeling as though we need to convince others—or have them convince us—of an absolute truth. This *quality of behaviour* can only exist because of a mutual agreement to listen without judgement, which requires an understanding of the subjective nature of personal experience.

"Cognitive dissonance is the state of tension that occurs when a person holds two cognitions, two ideas, attitudes, beliefs, or options that are psychologically inconsistent. Holding two ideas that are contradictory is very uncomfortable for humans and so humans will seek to resolve the two.

Human behaviour is predicated on a desire to eradicate cognitive dissonance by believing in the rightness of all our actions." [068]

~ Suzannah Lipscomb

Freyja, Óðinn, and Seiðr

The *Poetic Edda* is a collection of minstrel poems that would have been passed on from one singer to the next. One of these poems, *Lokasenna*, tells us that Vili and Vé had an affair with Óðinn's wife, Friggé/Freyja.

"This is taken by Grimm as reflecting the fundamental identity of the three brothers, so that Friggé might be considered the wife of either. According to this story, Óðinn was abroad for a long time, and in his absence, his brothers acted for him." [069]

Freyja was originally a fertility goddess of the Vanir. She accompanied her father, Njord (Poseidon), and twin brother Freyr (Mars), when they were selected to live with the Æsir, as part of the truce that ended the Great War between the two pantheons.

Freyja brought with her to Asgard, knowledge of Seiðr, *"a form of pre-Christian Norse magic and shamanism concerned with discerning and altering the course of destiny by re-weaving part of destiny's web."* [070]

Óðinn, ever in the pursuit of knowledge, learns Seiðr from Freyja, despite Seiðr being considered a feminine pursuit amongst the warrior gods of the Æsir.

"The Norns are the foremost masters of Seiðr. However, much gods, humans, and other beings may alter destiny, its initial framework is established by the Norns. To do this, they use the same means as any norn (Old Norse for "witch") . . . weaving, carving runes, and other mainstays of the toolkit of pre-Christian Germanic magic." [070]

~ Daniel McCoy

Tolerance

To remain in our ideal state, we must surround ourselves with people who nurture our thirst for perspective and can deliver perspective without judgement. If you only surround yourself with people who agree or argue with everything you say, your perspective will be significantly limited.

We must be free to ask questions. This is how we will discover the perspective of others. Questions should be asked with the intention of gaining perspective. It is your response-ability to ensure others feel at ease with your questions/inquiries. Ease must be established or you will never generate the confidence to inspire honest answers. Honest answers inspire exponential growth.

It is necessary to understand that perspective creates a greater awareness of consciousness. This allows us to evolve a unique perspective without needing to agree with others, or feeling threatened with an alternate perspective. We can then agree that cookie-cutter philosophy, capable of solving every crisis or conflict, does not exist.

As we rise above the superficial, we become free to realize the fullness of our authenticity.

Remaining teachable is the foundation of Self-knowledge.

Our First Time

Our first object-oriented experience of polarity is the observation of parents and siblings. Even their absence is an experience. These experiences shape how we relate to motive and emotive poles. How these experiences relate to one another is the factor that determines the organization of your fourfold personality.

My two parental influences were religion and law. While religion is totalitarian, law is democratic. Both are rooted in monotheism, though, so it was more like having two versions of the same thing—like a two-party political system.

On one side of this monotheistic coin, we have the "shoot first" mentality of religion, that obliges one to defend their assumptions at all costs. We may relate this to **fundamentalist behaviour** within any religion or political movement.

On the other hand, the justice system is compelled, at least theoretically, to take into account another point of view before casting judgement. Subjective experience is transmuted into objective fact based on the decision of a judge or jury.

Both systems create absolutes based on precedent and divine election.

"Complexes are part and parcel of who we are. The most we can do is become aware of how we are influenced by them and how they interfere with our conscious intentions. As long as we are unconscious of our complexes, we are prone to being overwhelmed or driven by them. When we understand them, they lose their power to affect us. They do not disappear, but over time, their grip on us can loosen."

~ Daryl Sharp

Anima/Yin ~ Animus/Yang

In Jungian psychology, Anima refers to the feminine/Yin characteristics inherent within man, and Animus refers to the masculine/Yang characteristics inherent within females.

The terms Anima and Animus are psychological terms that refer to *qualities of behaviour* within specific biological systems.

Yin energy is, by nature, emotive, while Yang is motive.

The shadow side of sympathy-oriented emotive/Yin energy is the tendency to become superficial, as in a broken legal system where sympathy is exchanged (consequences avoided) for financial gain.

The shadow side of solution-oriented motive/Yang energy is the *dictatorship tendency* to stubbornly refuse any perspective that threatens the belief systems on which we have constructed identity, regardless of demonstrable truth. This is the fundamentalist whom Nietzsche recognized would consciously embrace their illusion.

Awareness of polarity and a willingness to facilitate a balance of power empowers us to sidestep subconscious, habitual behaviour that does not support our ideal state. This allows us to consider the most effective way to communicate, and proceed with the confidence that accompanies Self-knowledge.

Polarity may be understood as the motive or emotive pole; the evaluative and the perceptual. Along with their respective shadows, we discover the fourfold nature of personality.

The symbol of the cross (+), popular beyond the Christian religion as a reference to the sacred, is a symbol of this fourfold nature, with the essence of what we may refer to as the authentic Self, or the ideal state, contained within the center point—the **source point**—from which all experiences emerge. This source point of psyche, giving way to the four directions, is a symbol of the pleroma "original state," Ginnungagap—the "yawning void."

Ideal state is a term that allows us to distinguish between the physical body and the essence that occupies it. Our bodies are a projection of psyche, and the objective world is an extension of our senses.

Object identification begins early, as you will recall, and is the foundation for our developing ego.

If an alien species saw an astronaut floating in space, they may mistake the suit for the person inside.

Our bodies are the suit *being* is wearing. The human suit provides a means for being to have a physical experience. Even more, our bodies may be understood as a battery that facilitates communication between *being* and the "yawning void," from which all created life proceeds.

Primary dialogues are as interchangeable as your wardrobe, although we tend not to change them as often. This can be helpful or unhelpful, depending on what holds your attention.

By directing our attention towards a specific, concentrated goal, we can achieve anything.

It becomes necessary to recognize the dialogues that compete for our attention, so we may adjust the objects of our thought to support our ideal state.

Our relationships are a projection of archetypes within. By observing others, we experience *qualities of behavior* without being possessed by them. From this fourth perceptual position, we become wandering Óðinn, seeing aspects of himself through the experiences of others. As a result of this observation, we may begin to adjust our behaviour to reflect our ideal state. This often means removing all distractions, as Óðinn did at this stage.

Intentional distractions are called **pattern interrupts**. These are strategic decisions to break our mental state with the intention of returning to our desired object of thought with fresh perspective.

The mind is eager to create solutions, and fresh perspective allows us to examine ourselves through a new set of eyes.

We are completely responsible for our knowledge and our ignorance.

We learn by experience and repeated behaviour.

The way you treat others is intrinsically linked to the way you relate to aspects of yourself. How ego relates to Anima//Animus is a reflection of how ego relates to the opposite gender. How ego relates to Self is a reflection of how ego relates to the object-oriented world.

Challenge 7: Discover Your Counter-Sexual Personality

Purpose: How I treat the opposite sex is a response to my relationship with Anima//Animus.

Tools: Audio Recorder, Notebook, Pen

Instructions: Begin with your audio recorder and talk about how you relate to the opposite sex. Can you identify a weakness in your own gender? Can you identify a weakness is the other? What makes these qualities of behaviour a weakness? Are you irritated, or do you exploit this weakness to get what you want?

~8~

"Prior to the cognitive revolution, humans were no different than any other animal. They had biology, but not history. History began with the cognitive revolution." [071]

~ Yuval Noah Harari

Life is filled with distractions. The pressure we put on ourselves to meet the expectations of others leaves us with little time to invest in ourselves. We have even managed to reframe Self-respect to induce feelings of guilt that we associate with selfishness.

Selfish has been defined: ***"(of a person, action, or motive) lacking consideration for others; concerned chiefly with one's own personal profit or pleasure."*** [072]

The problem with this definition is that it is entirely subjective. Who, exactly, is going to determine if my actions "lack consideration for others?" Who can determine my "chief concern" better than me?

Individuals must *ask themselves* if their actions lack consideration for others. This is introspection, though introspection is not mentioned in this definition, or any others I could find because we use the word "selfishness" as an adjective.

By making nouns more specific, we, necessarily, instigate a separation between two or more subjective experiences, which leads to judgement.

Is it even possible to not act selfishly? If someone feels good helping another, is that not selfish? How can we frown upon selfishness when we champion capitalism? Perhaps we misunderstand the term completely. I am not so sure that lacking consideration for others is synonymous with being my own "chief concern."

Our ancestors relied on the participation of each member of the community. If someone failed to contribute, or stole, or horded, they could be banished from the community, which was a sure precursor to death.

Patriarchy has gradually replaced community interests with the greed inherent to capitalism. The great majority are left feeling that their survival depends on looking out for themselves—an objective of patriarchy. Institutions we formerly relied on for providing us with absolute truths, are dissolving into ashes that reek of the betrayal we feel at having been so intentionally misguided.

Týr/Vili and Cognition

Týr, or "Tiw" in Old English—from where we get "Tiw's Day"—is one of the twelve principle deities of Norse mythology and sits on one of the thrones of Asgard. We may also consider the twelve Olympians of Greek mythology, and the twelve disciples.

Týr was father of the gods in Indo-European tradition, the most likely "all father" of the Vanir. Following the migration of Indo-Europeans, the second pantheons emerged. Týr is replaced by Óðinn (Zeus in Greece), and is considered to be of the Æsir. No attempt is made to associate Týr and the Vanir, as Christianity sought to "erase" the influence of the Indo-European paganism from "civilized" society.

This same genocide continues to this day. One need only search for credible information on the Indo-Europeans to confirm the extent at which accessibility to this information is discouraged to the "common man."

Try searching for books on Indo-Europeans, or anything by Georges Dumézil, a comparative mythologist.

The more expensive the book, the more you can be certain that it contains information that presents a compelling alternative to the working narratives as endorsed by modern society.

"With his (Týr) sacrifice ... not only procures the salvation of the gods but also regularizes it: he renders legal that which, without him, would have been pure fraud."

~ Georges Dumézil

Reclaiming a Lost Inheritance

Mindfulness, as represented in both the Buddhist tradition and Western medical interpretation, encourages a non-judgemental recognition of thoughts as being the imperative condition required for achieving inner harmony and maintaining a state of internal peace.

Many of us are becoming vaguely aware that life as we know it—or have believed it to be—is about to shatter. Bringing these unconscious assumptions into universal consciousness—Universal Individuation—has already begun and is facilitated by the energy created from our personal journeys.

This process of Universal Individuation is upon us. It will transform our world in the coming decades, as incredibly as the industrial revolution, the renaissance, the invention of the printing press, the wheel, and boats. This event—known as the Singularity—will be as dramatic as the discovery of fire.

The **Singularity** is the point at which technology becomes Self-aware. This is the next step in the cognitive revolution.

As creation (Homo sapiens) begins to create (artificial intelligence), our consciousness will organically evolve in tandem with what we are synthetically creating. From this fifth perceptual position, all other perceptual positions will seem obsolete.

Ego attempts to manufacture this "superiority" but is completely incapable of achieving this.

Skills may be developed, although they are always a pale facsimile to those who are "gifted" and tap into the universal creative energy—the Mozart's and the Van Gough's. These are the ones who create works that are timeless. They are not duplicators, but innovators. They do not copy, but are copied. These are The Overmen.

Times Are Changing

The dialogue of *Regressions* weaves through tenses and constantly changes perceptual positions as the reader becomes cognizant of the patterns that exist between our alternating experiences within the timestreams. These experiences—like all the archetypal templates—are designed to engineer the Individuation process.

As an awareness of the inconsistencies contained within incubated belief systems continues to grow, so does our desire to release ourselves from unconscious patterns and reclaim the inner source of power we have been trained to unconsciously outsource.

The world we grew up believing in, no longer exists. The more this becomes clear to us, the more this knowledge threatens the collective identity of those who cling to the fatalistic doctrine of divine election. The new regime recognizes the divinity of the individual; the democracy of humanity.

Ignorance Is Not Bliss

Throughout history, people have perished because of a lack of knowledge.

While traveling through Ethiopia with a group of anthropologists, I learned that many people *did not know* that being indifferent to flies on their face was causing blindness. I also learned that people were dying because they *did not know* that bathing, swimming, and doing laundry in the same water that animals defecated in was potentially life threatening.

Despite this, Eve is still condemned for her pursuit of knowledge in the Garden of Eden. Contrastingly, Óðinn is celebrated for his thirst for knowledge.

Ignorance is a powerful weapon that has incited countless atrocities. Ignorance is a belief in absolute truth, encouraged and supported, while not exclusive to, monotheism.

Absolute truth encourages discarding new information that may conflict with our established beliefs.

My grandmother never could have imagined the degree of change in the world she witnessed in her lifetime. I could say the same thing.

I never expected to see flying cars, colonization on mars, or autonomous artificial intelligence. I never expected to walk around with a computer in my pocket, or wear ear buds that could translate language, yet all of these technologies are, to some degree, in a stage of development. The marvels that will develop in the next forty years are too numerous to mention, and too unbelievable to plan for.

Out of all of the coming advancements, the one that really pushes me into the existential rabbit hole is genetic engineering. I never expected to have the option of not dying.

Genetic engineering is making huge, great strides towards life extension. If I see this happen and extend my life another fifty years, technology will have created some form of immortality. At the very least, by replacing the human experience with a synthetic or digital experience, where consciousness outlives Homo sapiens in a new digital vessel, to replace an organic one. The term "life extension" will become "digital consciousness experience (DCE)."

When that time comes, or in the years leading up to it, we will experience the death of (the concept of) God, as Nietzsche predicted. The Norse refer to this event in their mythology as Ragnarök, when the gods cease to exist.

If we can live forever, the concept of God becomes irrelevant. We don't need to worry about going to hell, so we don't try to impress God anymore, which means a transformation of morality and ethics. Hence, the emphasis Nietzsche placed on creating our own value and meaning within our experience, so that the wandering mind does not get lost amidst the outsourced beliefs that compete for our attention as primary dialogues.

Belief systems will crumble as our awareness evolves beyond the boundaries of constrained and contaminated systems of religion and government that currently dictate our *progressions* towards an enviable destiny—the one beyond subjective experience.

This is the journey towards Ragnarök that the Norse gods anticipated. The archetypes have been training at Óðinn's hall, preparing for the day when we must choose to surrender our lust for **absolute** certainty to the great "yawning void" of our uncertainties, from which our current aeon emerged.

After "Life"

We know nothing of the afterlife that is not completely subjective. The term itself—afterlife—is a bold assumption that something is waiting for our consciousness when body life ends.

All created things have some degree of consciousness and some degree of unconsciousness. The "I" you identify with as separate from the experience of others, is, necessarily, dependent on your physical body and the organs of your physical body that work together to create consciousness.

Consciousness exists within a vessel of specific parts (our triune brain), as though it is the heat from a stove element. If those parts break down, what happens to the heat/consciousness? Can it be produced independently in another vessel?

Regardless of whether I produce heat using a lighter or a match, the *quality of behaviour* of heat remains the same. There can be no argument that heat is not produced by fire. The only thing that has changed is the method of delivery.

The **method of delivery** indicates the probable means by which the substance produced will be used. The container of this method may even restrict the way in which the substance produced can be used.

We may think of psyche as the stovetop burner, and consciousness as the heat.

Consciousness is predicated upon the container or vessel holding it. All created things have a measure of consciousness, limited only by the capability of the form that carries it.

To suggest that consciousness, as it is manifested in the physical body, will remain in its current form, is to place the expansion of consciousness in a glass jar.

To assume our experience of consciousness—while contained within the human suit—will remain intact when it transitions from this container to an unknown one, is extremely presumptuous of us.

Therefore, we must eliminate the notion of an afterlife as a credible "fact," and simply admit that we do not know what will happen next.

Admitting what we do not know is the first step in resolving our existential "crisis," or "curiosity," with the unknown. This is the beginning of our journey to acquire the knowledge necessary to transcend reason-based, engineered philosophies designed to ensnare us within systems.

Systems of reason will never be able to explain the unknowable because it is not in our nature to know.

The expansion of consciousness has been a drawn-out process, and the next consciousness evolution may skip over Homo sapiens, just as it did with the Neanderthals, before us. It may evolve spontaneously and organically with the synthetic "creation" of Self-awareness in technology.

This precedent for quantum entanglement has been suggesting a measurable way, theorized by the hundredth monkey effect.

Each of us contains, within us, a portal to the creative potential of Ginnungagap—Universal Mind. The solar plexus is the organ of Universal Mind.

The subconscious is located in the cerebellum, and the organ of the subconscious mind is the sympathetic nervous system—one of the two main divisions of the automatic nervous system, which is responsible for our fight-or-flight (or freeze) impulse.

From the cerebellum, subconscious beliefs travel down our spine where they encounter the solar plexus and the creative potential of the "yawning void," from which all life emerges.

If we want to consciously access the creative potential of Universal Mind, we must "reprogram" the subconscious. This requires awareness of subconscious beliefs, a willingness to discard unsupportive belief systems, and the initiative to introduce new narratives with the intention that these narratives will encourage habitual behaviour that supports our ideal state. Habitual thought and behaviour is, then, taken up by the subconscious, which is communicated to Universal Mind.

This is the method by which we drink the cup of wisdom necessary to achieve fifth perceptual awareness and become true masters of our destiny. If we neglect, or, are unwilling to actively participate in this ongoing process, we will become inferior to developing technology, emasculating our chance for survival. We become modern Neanderthals, and we all know how that worked out.

I invite you to imagine how our ethical perspective is bound to change when the conditions for our survival depend upon asking a completely new set of questions.

Answers to these questions will demand *qualities of behaviour* that, first, synthesize, and then transcend, both sympathy *and* solution. A fifth perceptual position observes the functions of evaluative and perceptual poles, it does not rely on either.

Forward thinking—innovation—considers the outcome of our thoughts and actions before they are brought forth into existence. This allows us to anticipate consequences.

There is no need to adjust ourselves if our subconscious is working for us to produce ideal-state conditions.

Fifth perceptual thinking will provide us with a strategic "advantage" in the decades to come, as life becomes synonymous with consciousness.

A New Sacrifice

Ethics are fluid and constantly change. The concept of sacrifice is a good example. Sacrifice has always played a role in the development of spiritual practice, be it human or animal sacrifice. Symbols do not change, only our interpretation/conception of them.

Sacrifice, for the most part, is currently understood as service. We sacrifice our time.

Food is also a sacrifice. Our bodies are the temple. When we eat, food is consumed by the "fire" in our belly.

Persephone's Return

A primary agenda of the "old regime" has been to refine and redefine what is considered "civilized behavior," by eliminating all traces of Vanir consciousness, which is unconscious by nature. That the source of creative potential originates within the unconscious may seem ironic, but such is polarity.

When ego and Anima//Animus confront one another within the yawning void of Vanir consciousness, a fifth perceptual perspective will take form. For this to happen, we must recognize all functions of psyche—the Æsir (Animus) and Vanir (Anima) experience of consciousness, together with the fully-realized "divine child" of ego.

Knowledge of Vanir consciousness has been suppressed and hidden, therefore it may be considered occult. The Latin word, "*occultus*" means "clandestine, hidden, secret," therefore, occult knowledge is "knowledge of the hidden." [091]

As a child, I grew up believing that "occult" was another word for Satanism or evil. This kind of misinformation is typical of the "shoot first" mentality of the "old regime," who feel threatened by any knowledge that does not support the conclusions they want to believe. Why would anyone want to deny new information that could expand their experience? Because indoctrination—like incarceration—is profitable. Monotheism and capitalism support one another. They are two sides of the same coin.

We must rediscover the traditions of our ancestors and discover the unconscious experience.

This is the nature of Seiðr—a trance-like exploration of the collective unconscious—where we may extract value and meaning from the conditions we encounter in life in ways that are relevant to our personal experience.

Harmony within psyche facilitates harmony with Universal Mind. This secures our relationship with a universe who is friendly, where life unfolds *for* us, and we become co-creators of an experience to be enjoyed.

Anima—as an archetype for the unconscious—is the mediator between psyche and the unconscious, until we become fifth-perceptually aware. At this point, we begin creating symbols that communicate value and meaning to others. Realizing the inherent creative potential of our ability to think enriches our life experience. By adjusting our thought, we adjust our feeling. The degree that we *feel* our ideal state, is the degree to which we will experience it.

Prop-aganda

Propaganda is designed to control large numbers of people by creating a unified ideology that transcends culture and individuality. Knowledge threatens this agenda, as does cultural identity, and the sacredness of a place beyond the walls of dogma and institution.

Our resistance to progress develops from a perceived threat to identity and morality.

The best way to annex a tribe, community, or culture is to slowly introduce revised meaning and value to their existing symbols, gods, and traditions. Within a generation or two, the original meaning will have become lost.

Mistletoe, in the Norse tradition, was symbolic of ritual castration.

The swastika is an ancient religious symbol of the Indian subcontinent.

We may also consider major holidays of the year, which have their origin in pagan holidays. The Romans Christianized these holidays and gave them knew meaning, to the extent that the great majority are ignorant that Eostre was a pagan fertility goddess. [073] Her rebirth is also celebrated as Persephone's return from the underworld, Romanized by Christ's descent into Hades between "Good Friday" and "Resurrection Sunday."

It is both humorous and ironic that the symbol of the cross upon which Jesus died evolved from the phallic symbol of the May Pole (Pole Dancing), used to celebrate fertility between the pagan festivals of Ostara/Ēostre (Easter), and Beltane (May 1st).

"The biographies of saviors are symbolic of the meaning of the saviors teaching . . . it has nothing to do with what happened in life, it has to do with the implications of life."

~ Joseph Campbell

Ignorance reinforces our illusions, while knowledge liberates us from the "garden" of patriarchy.

As we approach a new paradigm shift in the evolution of consciousness, the "old regime" is grasping at straws to sustain their power over the thoughts/attention of the great majority, as reflected in our "education" system of misinformation, and our growing disdain for public education and libraries. The "old regime" understands that the way people think impacts their perception and response/reaction of the conditions they encounter in the world.

One of the most important documentaries you may ever watch is called *The Century of Self*, a BBC ***"documentary about the rise of psychoanalysis as a powerful means of persuasion for both governments and corporations."*** [092]

Into Eternity

The Tech Revolution has emasculated the deceptive potential of the old regime. Each one of us must assume response-ability for our knowledge *and* our ignorance.

The "hierarchy" of world power is changing once again. The industrial revolution opened the doors for modern capitalism, which allowed the "common man" to become the new aristocracy of the market economy. Capitalism upstaged the church, which, itself, had challenged the authority of the Royal families for the loyalty, attention, and finances of "the" people.

Cultural and geographical borders do not confine capitalism, nor the church. While the forms have changed, the symbols have not.

Places of worship, Houses of Parliament, and courtrooms are all designed after the Royal courts of medieval kingdoms, which, themselves, were fashioned after the Neolithic Longhouse [089] —a symbol of governance that is as universal as any of the Elementary Ideas.

The forces that will govern our **new world** will be completely unlike what we have experienced in the past. As we become more reliant on technology to maintain conditions of comfort, it seems plausible that we will turn to this technology to govern us, especially if it/they prove(s) more capable of achieving what the human condition has been unable to deliver—peace, equality, etc.

When technology surpasses us in innovation, we are sure to become the next endangered species.

We are actively developing an intelligence that will be superior to our own. One that will, no doubt, recognize the foolishness of our petty disputes, narrow-minded bias, and potential for mass destruction.

Of all these species within the biosphere we call earth, Homo sapiens are the greatest threat to the survival of all forms of life. This should humble us, yet it has failed to impress us more than the potential of capitalism to facilitate pleasure.

"Get Out of Here"

Do your actions support your ideal future, or are your words merely a gesture of some worthless idealism, adrift upon swells of progress you are unable to contain?

I asked a Zapatista soldier, in Mexico, if she believed they could win against the forces of neo-liberalism and the policies of globalization.

"I wouldn't be fighting if I didn't think we would win," she replied.

In a world of subjective battles and tongue-tied reasoning, there are no definitive winners and losers. Everyone you meet is just another sinner, and everywhere you go is just another hell. [074]

Challenge 8: Create an 18-Point index

Purpose: I will cultivate big-picture thinking and a fourth perceptual position.

Tools: Audio recorder, notebook, pen

Instructions: Create an 18-point index, as though you were planning on writing an autobiography. How will you tell your story? It will be helpful to categorize significant events. These, in turn, may become your index points that form the context for understanding your experience as a living mythos.

~9~

In the 1940's, the rivalry between two Swedish runners produced three new world records for the time it takes to run a mile. For nearly a decade, it was believed that the human body was physically incapable of running the mile faster than 4:01 minutes.

Then, on May 6, 1954, an English runner named Roger Bannister attempted the impossible. Trackside, doctors waited nervously with bottles of oxygen, ready to administer to Bannister when his lungs inevitably collapsed.

As it turns out, the oxygen would not be necessary, and Bannister completed the four-minute mile in 3:59.4 minutes.

Two months later, Bannister achieved this again, alongside Australia's John Landy.

Today, the four-minute mile is a common training milestone, even amongst high school students. What was impossible yesterday, becomes the new standard of tomorrow.

Impossibility is a state of mind. Innovators think beyond the norm and reach into what they believe to be possible instead of reaffirming the standards of others.

The creative power of our imagination (fifth perceptual) transcends the limits and impossibilities of the beliefs held to be absolute by the great majority.

Hnefatafl is a war strategy game popular amongst the Vikings. Played on a chess-like board, a single "King" is positioned in the middle of the board, surrounded by twelve warriors, who move like rooks in modern chess.

Twenty-four warriors, six on each side of the board, outnumber the King and his warriors. The object of the game is to reposition the King to one of the four corners of the board before the opposition kills him. This is achieved by flanking either side of an opponent.

The purpose of strategy games is to train the mind to think of possibilities.

"We now believe that the universe is vibrating, and that there are vibrations of different universes right here in this room. There is the universe of dinosaurs—because the comet never hit 65 million years ago. There is the wave function of aliens from outer space looking at the rubble of an earth that already was destroyed, all in your living room, except we have de-cohered from them; we're no longer in tune with them. We don't vibrate with them; therefore, our universe is tuned to one frequency . . . It means there are probably other parallel universes in your living room, and, believe it or not, this is called modern physics. Now, we don't like to tell . . . first year students about parallel universes because it would upset them . . . this is the modern interpretation of the quantum theory that many worlds represent reality." [075]

~ Michio Kaku

Mímir/Vé and Inspiration

Mímir, "The Rememberer," is an ancient being who existed at the creation of the world. He is believed to be a giant—the Greeks would have referred to him as one of the Titans.

Mímir was the being whom Óðinn sacrificed an eye for a sip of water from **Urðarbrunnr**, the "well of fate."

"More than any other being in Norse mythology, Mímir seems to be regarded as the divine animating force behind the wisdom of past tradition and its indispensable value as a guide for present actions.

His wisdom is the wisdom of the traditions that the heathen Germanic peoples held to be sacred." [076]

~ Daniel McCoy

Like Týr, Mímir survived the migration from the old pantheon to the establishment of a second pantheon, although his experience was short-lived.

The second pantheon of the Æsir are not, entirely, new and unfamiliar gods. They are a collection of deities from assorted Indo-European, Germanic, and Scandinavian traditions in an attempt to create a centralized Norse, or "Northern," system. Modern scholars agree that no such centralized system operated before the Christian invasion.

The main difference between the Æsir and the Vanir was the warlike disposition of the Æsir, replacing the fertility significance of Vanir consciousness.

George Dumézil, the French comparative philologist, suggests the "war" between the Æsir and Vanir represents a rivalry between the gods of fertility and the gods of "cognition."

Conflict can be reduced to a transition between those who embrace change and those who resist it. The "old regime" of the Æsir are now the ones resisting because whatever happens next, the "gods" will no longer exist. New templates of experience will emerge as a new pantheon of "gods" arises from the ashes of patriarchy, birthed from the womb of Loki/technology.

As part of the truce that ended the Æsir-Vanir war, Mímir was sent to the Vanir, along with Hœnir. Snorri Sturluson tells us in the *Ynglinga Saga* that Hœnir was made a chief, and Mímir often gave him good counsel. However, it soon became apparent that without Mímir at his side, Hœnir was a simpleton. The Vanir—who had sent the best among them—felt cheated. They beheaded Mímir and sent the severed head back to Asgard.

Óðinn embalmed the head of Mímir and spoke charms over it, in the tradition of Seiðr, which he learned from the Vanir fertility goddess, Freyja.

"Mímir's head represents Self inquiry, Self investigation, and great wisdom. This would qualify him as a symbol of logical and philosophical mind or an excellent learning tool for fledging seiðus on the importance of deep (well) and personal investigation, personal inquiry, and painfully honest personal dialogue." [085]

~ Yngona Desmond

The practice of Seiðr, as practiced by the Vanir, was a form of magic that channeled the forces/gods of nature. *Galdr* is a form of magic developed in Iceland following the invasion of Christianity. It operates on the same premise/conclusion of the Leviticus priests and the Indian Brahmanas—that those performing ritual/sacrifice control the behaviour of the gods/nature and, consequently, become more powerful than these forces.

Down to the Teeth

By now you will have completed a mental list of your nine primary dialogues. If you need to pause to complete this list and commit it to paper, please do so, now.

Our primary dialogues are, ultimately, what we rely on for guidance when it comes time to respond or react to an unanticipated event. They feed us information and give us suggestions, which, ultimately, determine whether we respond or react. The ability to recognize these primary dialogues is vital to governing the *qualities of behaviour* that possess us.

Consciousness may be a byproduct of our biological system. Regardless of its origin, adjusting our biological system can alter states of consciousness.

We must become aware of the factors that may sabotage our ability to remain established in our ideal state.

"Just as we are all part of the universe, a universe exists within all of us. With its own intricate galaxies, solar systems, ecosystems, and landscapes, containing all the clues for our secret hopes and dreams. Forming a cosmic map that tells us who we are, our true purpose, and what we need to be doing right this moment." [064]

~ Yumi Sakugawa

It may come as a surprise to you that the human body is an ecosystem. Many micro-organisms colonize humans; the traditional estimate is that *ten times as many non-human cells as human cells inhabit the average human body.*

Some microbiota that colonize humans are commensal, meaning they co-exist without harming humans; others have a mutualistic relationship with their human hosts. Conversely, some non-pathogenic microbiota can harm human hosts via the metabolites they produce. [077]

The *reticular formation,* reticular activating system (RAS), or extrathalamic control modulatory system, is *"a diffuse network of nerve pathways in the brainstem connecting the spinal cord, cerebrum, and cerebellum, and mediating the overall level of consciousness."* [078] The RAS is responsible for regulating wakefulness and sleep transitions, and thus, **consciousness states are a reflection of the spectrum between wakefulness and sleeping.**

Safe to Shore

As we approach the conclusion of *Living Mythos*, take the opportunity to share what you have learned with others. This will be an important step in integrating the information you have read and experienced here, while completing the challenges.

Subjective experience takes on objective form with the spoken word.

Within days you will *feel* the influence of your words, as they begin to change your predominant mental attitude. Behaviour (including words) is *always* the cause, and the conditions in our life are *always* the effect. The only way to change an effect is to change the cause. We must begin to isolate the cause that is producing the effect, which is the whole point of pattern tracking.

The greater the investment in Self, the greater the return. This is because you are entirely in control of what thoughts you choose to give attention to.

Thoughts are like clouds. They arise from seemingly endless places, though can just as swiftly be dismissed by *conscious intervention*, if they do not support our ideal state.

Thoughts that we hold in our attention determine our subjective experience. This is how we master, or become mastered by, our inherent creative potential.

"Dreams ... are invariably seeking to express something that the ego does not know and does not understand." [#079]

~ C.G. Jung

Do you recall any dreams from last night? How about last week, or last month? If you engage in active dream recall—like keeping a dream journal—you can probably remember a few of your recent dreams.

Dream awareness is like waking-life awareness. The objects of our attention are crystallized in our memory; they are more easily accessible to recall. The more attention we direct towards recall, the greater the mastery.

Each time we engage in active **recall** (remembering), we add an insulating layer around the object of our attention. The more insulated the memory, the more efficiently the memory responds when we call upon it.

Reinforcement supports mastery. The question, then, becomes, what is it you have become a master of? What has become so habitual in your life that you make it look easy?

> *"Conscious mind is reasoning will. Subconscious mind is instinctive desire, the result of past reasoning will."* [#008]
>
> ~ Charles Haanel

We may consider these questions as much a warning as they are an encouragement. If our reasoning will is unsupportive of our ideal state, our unsupportive thoughts are taken up by the subconscious and will determine our default behaviour. Likewise, if our reasoning will supports our ideal state, our supportive thoughts are taken up by the subconscious and will determine our default behaviour. This is the method by which we become a master of the activities that occupy our time, for good or ill.

If you want to change how you feel (effect), change the way you think (cause). This requires incentive on your part and may not be easy, but it is possible as long as you have the capacity for conscious thought.

You may not determine every thought that comes to mind, but you can determine the thoughts you entertain and discard.

This is the source of all power.

The world, as we subjectively experience it, is a reflection of the thoughts we entertain. Thoughts indicate specific states of consciousness that possess us.

Our ideal state is like a blurry picture that becomes focused as we learn to concentrate our attention on the *qualities of behaviour* that are required to maintain it. Become so identified with your ideal state that you are conscious of nothing else.

We can achieve the conditions we desire in life when we begin to focus and hold our attention on thoughts and actions that support our ideal state. It really is that easy. So, what is keeping the great majority from emancipating themselves from mental slavery?

We want to proceed without having to sacrifice what we already have.

A Taoist monk travelled a long way to visit a great master. The master greeted the young disciple and offered him some tea. The master began pouring the tea until the cup was overflowing; yet he did not stop pouring.

The student became flustered and asked the teacher to explain himself. "You are like this cup," began the wise teacher. "There is no room inside of you to impart anything new."

It's time to discard what no longer supports our ideal state. If we remain ahead of the curve, we support the organic evolution of consciousness. This may be the final solution to either an inevitable synthesis with technology, or our "destined" elimination at the hands of our creation.

We may begin by investing our greatest commodity—time—into supporting the evolution of consciousness by creating and maintaining the ideal state. This is the experience of our greatest imagination.

Like the character in *Regressions* we have become aware that our lives are spent jumping from one version of ourselves to the next, and we are ready to make it stop, now.

When we begin to concentrate our attention towards a specific, single-minded state, we can cut through all obstacles like water through rock; we activate our inherent potential for unlimited empowerment.

CHALLENGE 9: Create A Living History

Purpose: A living history will provide me with a big picture context for understanding my experience.

Tools: Audio recorder

Instructions: Go year by year through your life. Talk about the highs and the lows of your experience. Refresh yourself on the dates. Match up your respective ages with the calendar years. Touch on anything you feel is significant. This exercise can take as long as you like, but should last a minimum of fifteen minutes per year.

The more you do this, the more detail you will uncover. If you are having difficulty, you may use annual events as an anchor, such as your birthday or any other annual significant date. Anchors make it easy to remember the details between them.

REMAIN AN OBSERVER. Hover like a bird over the situations.

Ragnarök

4

4

Ragnarök

"All the religious principles of Christianity are pagan. Therefore, when the religious forms disappear, their principles will be assimilated by the new religious forms of the future." [080]

~ Samael Aun Weor

As we become more aware of conditions around us, we must resist the urge to judge our "new" observations. You may become aware of *qualities of behaviour* originating from ego, family, your friends and co-workers. Newly-acquired skills of observation must NOT inspire judgement, or you won't have learned a thing.

The more you inspire judgement, the more others will judge you.

Judgement has a tremendous impact on our overall, predominant mental attitude. It would be best to cultivate non-judgement, and as you begin to express the qualities of non-judgement, others will return qualities of non-judgement to you. This is the method by which we may truly learn together.

As we become more **body aware**, you may begin to notice physical sensations that were, previously, beyond your awareness. It is important not to judge these, as psychical sensations are the origin of thought.

How we feel may determine how we think, which, in turn, determines how we feel *until* a **conscious choice** is made to liberate ourselves from any unconscious *quality of behaviour* responsible for perpetuating undesirable conditions.

By judging physical sensations as negative, you may create psychosomatic ill-ness. Munchausen syndrome is a disorder in which the individual claims to be suffering from an imaginary illness.

The "benefits" of imagined illness are called secondary gain, such as the attention we may feel neglected of in a "well" state. It may be that illness allows you to not go to work, or to avoid some other unpleasant situation. In extreme cases, people move beyond imagining illness and harm themselves to feed this addiction or generate additional sympathy. *Munchausen by proxy* is when people intentionally harm their children for attention.

We may discover that many of the unpleasant conditions in our life offer some form of secondary gain. By bringing the unconscious into consciousness, we may adjust our behaviour.

Ultimately, we are responsible for examining ourselves and making decisions that will support our ideal state. No one can tell you what your ideal state must be.

My Head is an Animal

"In **The Origin of Consciousness and the Breakdown of the Bicameral Mind,** *Julian Jaynes suggests that ancient man possessed a bicameral mind, in which the temporal lobes of the brain were interconnected across the anterior commissural between the two hemispheres. So, these people would have heard 'voices' like a schizophrenic does and would have driven to take actions accordingly. The heroes in Greek myths, he said, heard the right and left hemispheres of the brain perform different functions...*

Jaynes suggests the ability to hear voices was lost abruptly by most people at more or less the same time, so people would have felt the gods had abandoned them. Those who retained the ability to 'hear' would then have been sought out as soothsayers.

Today, we are largely stranded in the side of our brain that thinks with structure and logic, cut off from the gifts of the other side—instinct, inspiration, and mystical knowledge—although we still possess them." [#081]

If the inner dialogues of the archetypes were audible and projected themselves in a kind of waking hallucination, then polytheism would make perfect sense.

Following the "abandonment of the gods," the archetypes no longer spoke audibly. Internal dialogues are now siphoned through a solitary voice (monotheism), so that we are unable to distinguish one from another without taking the **incentive** to do so.

Individuation liberates us from this discordant choir of internal dialogues by supporting our ability to distinguish these voices.

In doing so, we become a participant in the conditions of our life, instead of being manipulated by an entire cast of archetypes we mistakenly assume to be originating from the same source, with the same appetites, personalities, and goals.

Our choices reflect the inner dialogues that hold our attention. These *qualities of behaviour* determine our predominant mental attitude.

Polytheism would have developed quite naturally from pantheism, which regards all of creation as an expression of the divine. The conditions of the earth necessitate the survival of life. Nature could just as easily reduce the chances of life to thrive, thus the idea of nature as a god is completely sensible to people who were, quite literally, held captive by the forces of nature.

"When you are a nomadic people, your worship has to be that which is everywhere."

~ Joseph Campbell

All organs and systems of the body are members of the same team and should work together in harmony to create and sustain a thriving living system. This is the philosophy of pantheism.

Pantheism could have been the first philosophy to emerge from the cognitive revolution, as Homo sapiens sought meaning to account for Self-awareness. I can only imagine this "awakening" would be like waking up in a foreign environment, yet having some vague recollection of which direction to go for water.

The idea that a river is a gift from some divine source, and that the Sun may be *the* divine source, would make a lot of sense because your entire existence depends on these forces of nature.

That life requires life to thrive may be the oldest existential dilemma. The Brahmanas—a collection of ancient Indian texts—explore the nature of sacrifice. They came to, essentially, the same conclusion as the Hebrews in the Old Testament book of Leviticus—that the priestly class, who administered the sacrifice, had power over how the god(s) would behave. This, in turn, meant the priests had more power than the gods, since they could manipulate their behaviour.

This idea is echoed in Galdr and forms the *left-hand path*—a term used to distinguish those who use ritual and sacrifice as a means to manipulate the *qualities of behaviour* of the "gods" throughout esoteric and occult thought.

In comparison, the right-hand path focuses on rituals designed to align us with the rhythms of nature and natural laws. Maintaining this harmony becomes the means by which we become co-creators, weaving our destiny from the template conceived by the Three Norns.

Understanding the spectrum between extremes supports our practice of moderation, and will ensure we do not get caught up in the tendency to shift like a pendulum when challenged by unanticipated conditions.

Extremes limit our ability to understand the true nature of the universal creative force from which all life has emerged.

By the time of Roman civilization, Government trumped the priestly class. Caesar was no longer chosen by God, he had become a living god. There was no separation of church and state.

Resolving polarity will be the next evolutionary step in the cognitive revolution. When we learn to moderate a harmonious relationship between the motive and emotive poles of nature and psyche, we move beyond our tendency to shift between extremes and discover our inherent potential to create.

This three-way harmony allows the creation of a fourth perceptual position, projected as wandering "one-eyed" Óðinn. Achieving this state is necessary for consciousness to organically develop a fifth perceptual position, where consciousness observes itself creating.

Polytheism and Monotheism

"The Odyssey is fundamental to the Western canon and is the second oldest extant work of Western literature. The Iliad is the oldest. Scholars believe the Odyssey was composed near the end of the 8th century BC, somewhere in Ionia, the Greek costal region of Anatolia." [082]

Socrates recognized the departure from classical mythology—the gods of *The Iliad and Odyssey*—and encouraged this move towards rationalism. The influence of the Indo-European migration into the high civilizations of Mesopotamia, Greece, and the Indus Valley introduced petition-oriented spiritual practices. They placed an emphasis on interpreting symbols, supported by an emerging monotheistic philosophy that arose with the development of mathematics and language to record celestial movements. The divine order of the cosmos replaced the nature-oriented forces of the earth. "God" did not exist in the earth, but beyond it, as expressed by the second pantheons of polytheism and the one, all-father of monotheism.

Plato carried this torch a little further with his conception of the "gods" as archetypal ideas, though Plato had to walk a thin line. There was still opposition to rationalism, and he had seen his teacher and mentor, Socrates, killed.

By the time Aristotle came into the picture, rationalism was establishing itself as the new paradigm in the West. Intellectuals were looking to distance themselves from the classic mythological worldview.

Monotheistic philosophy developed as a method to govern the mind, which placed ego as a kind of totalitarian dictator. Like Zeus, ego is unable to govern the archetypes/gods. This is not the role of ego, which is why ego has not been successful in this task.

Ego emerged from the unconscious to communicate objective experience to Self. Ego receives insights from the unconscious through the language of symbol.

Rationalism is, in essence, an attempt to interpret unconscious symbol and communicate that knowledge consciously.

If we consider the sixty-four hexagrams of the *I Ching* as templates for experience, and imagine siphoning all through one conduit to produce a discordant symphony, then we are a step closer to understanding the disharmonious state of psyche. The good news is that, in most cases, we have only to recognize the primary dialogues—of which there are only nine—to affect change within the "pantheon" or archetypal templates. This is because all of the templates of experience originate from the source point of Universal Mind, and are communicated to the "personalities" of our fourfold personality and their respective shadows. These nine "forces" become the "voices" of our primary dialogues. They reflect qualities of behaviour that support our predominant mental attitude, as determined by the objects of our attention.

Our ability to identify the primary dialogues that advise us is, necessarily, of great value in liberating ourselves from unconscious dialogues and impulses.

Ego is not meant to govern the archetypes, only to communicate the objective experience they provide to psyche and facilitate a harmonious relationship between Self and Anima//Animus. This is achieved by filtering experience through both the motive and emotive poles, instead of containing our experience to the leash of an extreme.

Pantheism is the language by which ego communicates subjective experience to the objective world. This necessitates equality, as every form of consciousness is an expression of creation from the same source: the unconscious.

As the archetype of the unconscious, Anima has a special relationship with the creative force from which all life has emerged.

Animus resents ego for this special relationship.

Symbols are so powerful because they contain the power of subjective experience. Institutions are a projection of our desire to replace subjective experience with absolutes.

A Way Back

Prior to the cognitive revolution, our hunter-gatherer ancestors lived in an unconscious state, unaware of their autonomy from the environment. The cognitive revolution began a slow evolution of consciousness that has continued to this very day.

Everything that has happened since the cognitive revolution has been motivated by a departure from an Anima state into an Animus state; from matriarchy to patriarchy.

It could be said that the cognitive revolution is the source point for patriarchy, and, consequently, the source point for man's elitism and women's resentment.

Harmony between Vanir and Æsir consciousness will give birth to a new level of consciousness that transcends the two modes of consciousness that predicate mental activity, conscious and unconscious. The fifth perceptual position is an archetype for this third form of mental activity that will emerge.

Elitism and resentment are *qualities of behaviour* expressed by, and through, immature ego—the high chair tyrant. Neither Self, nor Anima//Animus, is capable of expressing him or herself emotionally. Emotions are a function of ego. Ego reacts to its inability to govern the archetypes.

Until ego comes to peace with its role as interpreter of experience and moderator of the distribution for energy that mind creates by thinking, psyche will not fully develop, and will remain in an immature state.

Motive and emotive poles may be symbolically identified by Óðinn's ravens, Huginn and Muninn, and their shadows, Óðinn's wolves, Geri and Freki.

"From about 70,000 years ago, onwards, we begin to see continuous change in the technology of things like spear points. Every few thousand or hundreds of years, you have a new style of spear points, of knives... not only the invention of new technology, but the continuous improvement of all technology." #071

~ Yuval Noah Harari

Polytheistic mythology developed from pantheistic folklore, which reinvented itself when earth divinities began to be imagined from a celestial, cosmological perspective.

Sumerian civilization begins charting the skies around 3200 BCE. This signifies that the integration of patriarchy has reached a new level; a historical Pandora's box, from which there would be no return. This also means that matriarchy—symbolic of Anima—continued to remain the dominant force, despite the slow burn of evolving consciousness.

Even if patriarchy began to assert itself with the realization of man's role in procreation—only about 20,000 years ago—this still means matriarchy dominated for the first 50,000 years after the cognitive revolution.

Monotheism interprets the earth, and everything in it, as created and abandoned by a singular god. This was a departure from earlier Semitic beliefs, which include: a mother goddess known as Asherah, consort *"of Sumerian God, Anu; Ugaritic El, or Yahweh, the God of Israel and Judah."* #083

Because God abandoned the earth, it can be exploited.

The gods and goddesses were symbols, interpreted in culturally relevant ways. As ethnic folklore became more centralized, it also became more dogmatic. Political forces would have recognized the advantage of uniting the people under common moral and spiritual convictions.

By the time of Christianity and Islam, monotheism was beginning to replace polytheism as the main contender for expression of divinity in the West.

While Judaism and Islam borrow heavily from Sumerian and other culturally relevant traditions in Mesopotamia, Christianity is a near-identical facsimile of Zoroastrianism, which dominated the Indo-Iranian tradition.

While the influence of the Indo-Europeans emerged in the developing religions of the East and West, among Hinduism and Zoroastrianism, respectively and specifically, the religions of the East championed polytheism; perhaps because they continued to remain more nomadic than the emerging city-states and kingdoms of the West.

By the time of Socrates, circa 470 BCE, the characters of Homer's *The Odyssey* were beginning to be un-personified, and interpreted as ideas. The gods and goddesses were templates containing *qualities of behaviour* that expressed the human condition, although imagined in extraordinary ways.

If Jaynes [093] is correct, and the imagination was projected into the sense experience, Homo sapiens who lived 500 years before Socrates may have experienced the sensational reality of daylight hallucinations.

"We think of the sacred in terms bequeathed to us by the classical monotheistic religions we have been all too eager to shake off. That is, for something to be sacred, it must, in the monotheistic view, be objectively true and provide an absolute code of morality. It necessarily involves some doctrine of the One True Something and the one right way to live. While it has been sensible and in many ways helpful to reject this view, one cannot help but ask how much we have actually moved beyond it if we still insist on speaking of the sacred and profane in monotheistic terms." [084]

~ Daniel McCoy

For whatever reason, Homo sapiens (to our knowledge) were the only species affected by the cognitive revolution. This gave us an incredible tactical advantage over our enemies, who, consequently, were unable to learn from their mistakes. In battle, this advantage would have changed outcomes.

The degree of genocide mentioned throughout the Old Testament may allude to the massacre of Neanderthals, and "inferior versions" of *genus homo*. That the order to massacre comes directly from "God" may be understood as the *qualities of behaviour* we relate as the high chair tyrant.

The cognitive revolution will happen again, this next time, for artificial intelligence, in an event that is referred to as the **Singularity**—when machines become Self-aware and exceed our experience of consciousness.

In *The Singularity is Near*, futurist Ray Kurzweil estimates this event will happen by 2045. When it does happen, will Homo sapiens realize our destiny as the inferior species or will we discover some way to remain superior?

Generalizations Are Not Absolutes

Generalizations help us compartmentalize our thoughts. Generalizations are like putting thoughts into folders and knowing where each piece of information is located, instead of leaving all of your thoughts like a pile of papers on the table. One gust of wind and those papers will become even more mixed up.

The first rule of generalizations is they are not absolute. Generalizations that do not follow this rule become dogma.

Dogma contains the meaning you require to resolve the fact that in order for you to live, other life must perish. Both the animal and the vegetable kingdom are sacrificed so that our species may thrive. To resolve this, we require meaning.

The cognitive revolution gave birth to man's search for meaning, as expressed through our connection with the Universal Mind, the collective unconscious, mystical, Brahman, Tao, Numen, Subtle Non-Manifest, etc. [#034]

The Silence

Mindfulness of Breath Meditation asks us to consciously attempt to suppress thought, stepping into pure observation mode. You don't count breaths, you don't try to influence or change anything; simply observe.

The unconscious creative potential of Anima is represented by *the silence* that defines this style of meditation. This is a great way to cultivate your relationship with Anima in a healthy way. This is Anima in her natural state; unconscious potential or static mind; mind at rest.

Ego and Self must learn to quiet down.

Anima/Freyja is now represented as the fullness of the nurturing mother.

Our experience in life is a projection of archetypal templates brought into manifestation by our interaction with them. These templates take form as determined by the *quality of behaviour* we manifest in our thoughts and actions. When we take the incentive to infuse value and meaning within the conditions of our life, we become as the Brahmans and the Galdor practitioners, having understood ourselves to be "more powerful" than external forces that would, otherwise, control our destiny. By discovering the archetypal patterns that exist within all conditions, we become co-creators of our destiny. When we choose to respond instead of react to unanticipated situations, our authentic Self remains of the "priestly" class. Forethought becomes divination. Mythology is revealed as the owner's manual for consciousness.

"When people talk about mythology and rituals, they usually talk about it from the standpoint of modern mentality, and they speak

about finding the causes of the world, origin myths, and so forth—explanatory myths . . . what are called ethological myths.

That's not what myths are about. Myths do not have to do with analyzing and scientifically discovering causes; myths have to do with relating the human being to his environment." [086]

~ Joseph Campbell

Norse mythology evolved from the folklore of the **Teutons**, the Germanic branch of the Indo-Europeans.

Because the sources of Viking-Age mythology mainly come from during and following the Christian invasion, if we want to discover information about the original Pantheon, The Vanir, it is essential to examine the Teutons and the **Picts** of Northern Scotland. The Picts were, perhaps, the final ethnic group of the West to resist the Christian invasion. Unlike the Celts, the Picts did not convert to Christianity—they survived it, and integrated themselves into the new diversity that occupied Scotland following the migrations of the Vikings from Scandinavia, and The Celts from Ireland.

Each step forward in cognition was a step away from the nature-oriented ways of the Vanir, who Christendom—with its emphasis on reason—felt superior to and, consequently, justified to exterminate.

The Evolution of Consciousness

Our superior function offers us a glimpse into how we can participate in the evolution of consciousness.

The inferior function—directly opposite from the superior function—is the one most closely related to the unconscious. This will be the function of the personality that is least developed and yet manifests itself as shadow most regularly.

"The inferior function is practically identical with the dark side of the human personality." [087]

"The inferior function secretly and mischievously influences the superior function most of all, just as the latter represses the former most strongly." [088]

~ Carl Jung

The inferior function cannot rise up to meet the superior function, although by switching to a fourth perceptual position, we are able to access all aspects of our fourfold personality on an equal basis.

This fourth perceptual position is empowered by a conscious journey into the unconscious, which may be understood as the role of the Völva in the Seiðr tradition.

This is observation from a pure creative potential.

Meditation helps synchronize the brain, as do other activities that require the use of both brain hemispheres at the same time, such as playing a musical instrument, creating art, etc.

When we learn to consciously suspend thought, intentionally placing our superior function in alignment with our inferior function, judgement and Self-criticism evaporate.

969696969

Thoughts predicate our experience. What if all your thoughts projected as reality—the way they may have for the ancients?

Fortunately—or unfortunately—they do not.

This still happens during dreaming, though we are able to avoid a Pandora's box of consequences—or so we assume. It could be that dreams are a symbolic expression of what our consciousness is experiencing from within a dimension of reality, a dimension our consciousness is unable to currently experience.

We assume our dream theatre does not produce consequences in waking life, although it is more likely that we *are* influenced by the events of dreams, whether we consciously remember them or not. On one hand, this seems manipulative and on the other, liberating. It depends on whether you interpret the events of life as happening *to* you or *for* you.

The more I consider it, the more it seems that consequences in waking life result from the content of our dreams, just as surely as thoughts motivate behaviour.

The presupposition of dream work is that our dreams use the symbolic language of the unconscious to work through unresolved situations from daily life, so that we can discover the inherent meaning in our experiences. That this happens unconsciously does not alter the process.

We become more conscious of our experience by actively engaging in interpreting symbols in both sleeping and waking state. In this way, we bring the contents of the unconscious into conscious awareness.

"The symbol is only the outward form of the spiritual reality within, therefore unless we can possess the spiritual reality, the form disappears." [#008]

~ Charles Haanel

I Am a Living Mythos

Like sirens, we're constantly hypnotizing one another with our words. Every word is an intention we are voicing.

Become an observer of your speech. Analyze the intention of your words. When this practice becomes subconscious, language becomes a tool for *achieving* mastery.

This is the method by which habitual behaviour determines our experience.

The subconscious mind does not have the faculty of discrimination. It is up to the conscious mind to confirm the content of our thoughts, words, and actions support our ideal state.

Fear is any thought that threatens our ideal state. We must recognize the *qualities of behaviour* that lead to fear and eliminate them. We may do this by holding ideas big enough to counteract or destroy all petty and annoying obstacles.

"Anything that can be named or regarded as a form is a symbol." [086]

~ Joseph Campbell

It's not what you say that matters as much as what people hear. Effective communication is when another understands your intended meaning. When our attention (will) is divided, enthusiasm is compromised, along with our creative potential.

The power of creation originates within the inferior function. We mustn't neglect that which we do not understand, and we must not fear it. We must recognize our ignorance and discover healthy ways to give expression to undeveloped expressions of psyche—recognizing that all templates of behaviour have the potential to cultivate our ideal state.

We relate to our environment through pantheism—when we recognize the divinity in all forms of consciousness. It is up to each individual to resolve the issue of sacrifice in a way that is personally meaningful. Service is a modern example of sacrifice. Service allows us to sacrifice/invest our time to ease the suffering of others. This action creates harmony between Self and ego.

The stories we tell ourselves are rooted in our desire to embody the strength and beauty of our forgotten mythologies; a yearning for visions, projected into the objective world.

How shocked would you be if you woke up in thirty seconds and realized that everything that has happened in your life since you started reading *Living Mythos* had been a dream? What then?

> *"The final aim of the Northern Mysteries is the establishment of free and independent individuals and peoples; all sovereign and authentic within themselves.*
>
> *If the inner world of the soul is explored and understood, the gateways are opened to a greater understanding of the larger world."* [021]
>
> ~ Edred Thorsson

The Eleusinian Mysteries of ancient Greece contain incredible insights into the emergence of cognition.

According to the *Hymn to Demeter,* the earth goddess, Demeter, goes searching for her daughter Kore (Persephone), who had been abducted by Hades (Pluto), god of the underworld. The physical/objective world (the mother), has gone looking for the unconscious (the maiden), who has been abducted by consciousness. Persephone's separation and reunion with the unconscious is represented by her annual return form the underworld, celebrated at the beginning of the growing season.

Æsir consciousness replaced the Vanir unconscious state.

The "fall of man" from the paradise of Eden is represented as knowledge replacing ignorance.

Just as evolution builds upon a previous foundation, the evolution of concepts, ideas, and form, builds on itself, creating **value and meaning** that is relevant to culture and experience.

Awareness of our evolution creates the conditions for harmony, synchronizing the brain into one cohesive unit. As the Norse concept of destiny suggests, we have a role to play in the evolution of our consciousness, if we *choose* to participate.

When Nietzsche spoke of the death of God, he echoed what all the Norse gods were aware of.

Ragnarök signified the end of the gods. Óðinn would be consumed by the offspring of his own shadow, the great wolf, Fenrir—who may be understood as an archetype for the fifth perceptual position.

Consciousness creating consciousness is synonymous with consciousness destroying consciousness. This is the template woven throughout mythology. The good news is that whether consciousness destroys or creates will be determined by our initiative.

Whatever happens next, a new spiritual identity will emerge that will define the *progression* of consciousness into the next aeon. The next pantheon will not be outsourced to projected external forces or captive subjective ones.

Future generations will understand the sacred as demonstrable truth. Some will *develop* these new cognitive abilities organically; others will *acquire* them synthetically.

The same universal life force that keeps our hearts beating, co-ordinates unfolding conditions of life to synchronize with others. This allows us to share a collective, objective experience while retaining a subjective one, in which value and meaning are relevant to our personal experience.

When we experience the unfolding conditions of our lives as a *Living Mythos*, we recognize people and conditions as symbolic projections of universal experience.

We are responsible for our ability to co-create with the Universal Mind—the great life force out of which all things proceed.

Thought is spiritual energy, and our ability to think is our ability to act upon the Universal and bring it into existence.

This is the art of Self-realization.

Epilogue

"We used to think agriculture gave rise to cities and later to writing, art, and religion. Now the world's oldest temple suggests the urge to worship sparked civilization." [094]

~ Charles C. Mann

In June 2011, National Geographic published an article about the Neolithic stone circle *Göbekli Tepe*, in the Southeastern Anatolia Region of modern day Turkey.

This ancient sacred site has revealed no less than twenty renovations, spanning thousands of years, before it was eventually abandoned. The oldest of these was constructed using slabs of limestone that stood eighteen feet high; weighing sixteen tonnes. *Göbekli Tepe* would have been an awe-inspiring site to primitive hunter-gatherers. It is astonishing that a group of people who had no written language, metal, or pottery, had the engineering skill to erect such an elaborate temple.

"For reasons yet unknown, the rings at Göbekli Tepe seem to have regularly lost their power, or at least their charm. Every few decades, people buried the pillars and put up new stones—a second, smaller ring, inside the first . . . Bewilderingly, the people at Göbekli Tepe got steadily worse at temple building. The earliest rings are the biggest and most sophisticated, technically and artistically. As time went by, the pillars became smaller, simpler, and were mounted with less and less care. Finally, the effort seems to have petered out altogether by 8200 BC." [094]

History provides a key to unlocking our inherent potential because an understanding of the past gives us the context for appreciating our relevance in the present, and provides a template for envisioning where we may be headed.

The version of history we identify with must, necessarily, be updated, with the advent of new technology—like carbon dating—which allows us to accurately determine the origin of artifacts uncovered. For centuries, religious prejudice enforced a strict timeline on history that enforced overwhelming errors to support their narrative, implying Adam and Eve walked out of Eden and into ancient Greece, the pyramids were constructed by Hebrew slaves, and dinosaurs were either a myth, or existed for only a brief time about 5000-6000 years ago.

The contention between the religious and scientific communities—brother and sister to their patriarchal, monotheistic father—has only succeeded at keeping ignorant people distracted with the business of defending their idealistic opinions.

Distraction is the most effective means of control.

Idealism is engineered distraction intended to secure our attention to the degree that we become possessed with manufactured ideas and philosophies. Idealism keeps us running within an endlessly spinning wheel, which creates the illusion of value and meaning, pacifying our nature to seek answers beyond convention.

By attempting to solve the problems around us, we neglect the power of inner, autonomous transformation.

In Viktor Frankl's classic, *Man's Search for Meaning*, he reminds us that our attitude is always ours to curate or give away.

"Everything can be taken from a man but one thing: the last of human freedoms—to choose one's attitude in any given set of circumstances, to choose one's own way." [097]

~ Viktor E. Frankl

By outsourcing our attitude to others and/or belief systems we have acquired and feel compelled to defend, we have no attention remaining to consider an alternative to the Greco-Roman system.

"When Rome spread its empire over the whole Mediterranean and into part of Western Europe, care was taken to eliminate anything that might harm its socio-political organization. This is very evident in Celtic countries; the Romans pursued the Druids until they disappeared into Gaul and later into Britain. The Druids represented an absolute threat to the Roman State because their science and philosophy dangerously contradicted Roman orthodoxy. The Romans were materialistic, the Druids were spiritual. For the Romans, the state was a monolithic structure, spread over territories deliberately organized into a hierarchy. With the Druids, it was a freely consented moral order with an entirely mythical central idea. The Roman's based their law on private ownership of land, with property rights entirely vested in the head of the family, whereas the Druids always considered ownership collective. The Romans looked upon the women as bearers of children and objects of pleasure, while the Druids included women in their political and religious life. We can thus understand how seriously the subversive thought of the Celts threatened the Roman order, even though it was never openly expressed. The talent of the Romans in ridding themselves of the Gallic and British elites is always considered astonishing, but this leaves out of the account the fact that it was a matter of life or death to Roman society." [#095]

~ Jean Markale

It is easy to read the above description of the (Roman) Empire and immediately recognize what many of us *feel* is wrong with the world today.

If we do not begin integrating a neglected aspect of our collective psyche, then we—as a civilization and species—will disappear as surely as the (historical) Roman Empire did.

This brings us back to legacy, and the shift that happened when men realized they had a role in childbirth.

Creating legacy became an issue of immortality. "Duty" and "honour" were such important concepts to our ancestors who believed that if you could inspire future generations to *remember* you—to write and sing of the great things you did—that you would, in death, become a living myth within your respective tradition.

In **matriarchal** societies, value and meaning were understood to transcend the lifespan of an individual if their actions (in this life) could impact the lives of their *community* in future generations.

In **patriarchal** societies, value and meaning were understood to transcend the lifespan of an individual if *his* actions (in this life) could impact the lives of *his offspring* in future generations.

Power and prestige became inherited, not earned, regardless of whether the offspring were worthy or prepared for the responsibility, which accounts for the reliable incompetence that results from those who hold a measure of power who never had to earn it.

It is refreshing to discover The Giving Pledge, comprised of some of the wealthiest of today, who have chosen to end this patriarchal tradition by pledging their wealth to philanthropy.

As men began to shift away from community values and towards building "kingdoms of this world," this, necessarily, led to the appropriation and possession of land, the domestication of animals, and slavery, to aid him in this pursuit.

As living beings, *Homo sapiens* are the ultimate creator of our experience because we have the ability to make choices based on forethought. This is the "forbidden fruit" of knowledge. The Neolithic Revolution was the beginning of the evolution of consciousness. We are free to think and act independently of instinct and convention, if we so choose.

The **hero's journey** is our quest to discover true freedom from the entanglement of our biological evolution. This is the Great War between flesh and the mind that we all must wrestle, as Jacob did at the foot of heaven's stairwell—the proverbial dragon slayed by Lancelot.

It is worth noting that in the story of Jacob the angel—upon realizing he could not defeat Jacob–dislocated his hip out of joint. [099] This may be understood to reference women; specifically, the "pain of childbirth," which was God's curse upon Eve for eating the fruit of the knowledge of good and evil, something Empire wanted to discourage. After all, **ignorance** begets distraction.

It is also interesting to note that Jacob later names the location of this wrestling match, Penuel, or "I have seen the face of God." Could the French word, pineal—of which the pineal gland receives its name—be a reference to the same intended meaning of this biblical myth?

Pinéal comes from the Latin *pinea* "pine cone," from the root *pinus* "pine tree," which leads us back to the symbolism of the world tree—a dominant **elementary idea** woven throughout worldwide mythology.

In the Völuspá, [085], perhaps the oldest known pagan document available to the general public, we learn that the first two humans—*Askr* "ash tree," and *Embla* "elm tree"—were created by the gods out of tree trunks that washed ashore from the great primordial waters.

It is widely believed amongst Indo-European Shamanic and pagan traditions that mankind emerged from *within* trees—not a great leap from the ongoing theory of evolution, which suggests man climbed down from the branches of trees.

A Proto-Indo-European basis has been theorized for the duo based on the etymology of *Embla*, meaning "vine." In Indo-European societies, an analogy is derived from the drilling of fire and sexual intercourse. Vines were used as a flammable wood, where they were placed beneath a drill made of harder wood, resulting in fire.

Jaan Puhvel comments; *"ancient myths teem with trite 'first couples' of the type of Adam and his by-product Eve. In Indo-European tradition, these range from the Vedic Yama and Yamī and the Iranian Mašya and Mašyānag, to the Icelandic Askr and Embla, with trees or rocks as preferred raw material, and dragon's teeth or other bony substance occasionally thrown in for good measure."*[101]

In his study of the comparative evidence for an origin of mankind from trees in Indo-European society, Anders Hultgård observes that *"myths of the origin of mankind from trees or wood seem to be particularly connected with ancient Europe, Indo-Europe, and Indo-European-speaking peoples of Asia Minor and Iran. By contrast, the cultures of the Near East show almost exclusively the type of anthropogenic stories that derive man's origin from clay, earth, or blood by means of a divine creation act."*[102][100]

We may begin to see the Druids, not as they have been reinvented in modern times as an agent of the strange and archaic, but as a historically relevant expression of a matriarchal society; an alternative to the Abrahamic/Aristotelian narrative that dominates Western thought.

I am not suggesting that we return to matriarchy—which would be no better than a pendulum shift to another extreme. Rather, by recognizing Anima as an archetype for matriarchy, and Animus as an archetype for patriarchy, we may begin to harmonize these two poles of collective consciousness.

This would lead to Individuation on a collective level, a process that will become exponential when ten percent of the world's population intentionally embraces Individuation as a tool for personal transformation.

Research by scientists at RPI's Social Cognitive Networks Academic Research Center (SCNARC), published an abstract in the journal *Physical Review E* to support this figure.

"When the number of committed opinion holders is below ten percent, there is no visible progress in the spread of ideas. It would literally take the amount of time comparable to the age of the universe for this size group to reach the majority.

Once that number grows above ten percent, the idea spreads like flame."[103]

The role of ego in personal and collective transformation—a result of the ongoing process of Individuation—cannot be understated. Ego's function within psyche is magnified when it is projected onto the collective unconscious and conscious theatre, which is to say that ego must mature from its high chair tyrant stage, manifest as patriarchy into a fully-realized *Divine Child*, in which the poles of matriarchy (Anima), and patriarchy (Animus), are synchronized. It is only when this has been achieved that our species will rise above the inherent suffering that results from its sickly fascination with extremes.

Free will is the Ability to Think

Pelagius was an Irish ascetic moralist accused of attempting to revive the Druidic philosophy of nature and free will.

"Pelagius' argument was that human beings had free will, while Augustine believed in predestination." [098]

~ Peter Berresford Ellis

Predestination claims that all events are willed by God—a doctrine that allows the church to justify the suffering of their congregations to the congregations.

Calvinism further suggests that, despite predestination, "divine knowledge" is bestowed upon the leaders of the church/monarchy, granting them the special privilege of interfering in God's unfolding plan of predestination to secure their will/desires, while alleviating any personal responsibility or accountability to, otherwise, explain themselves. This theology harkens back to the priestly class of the Levites (Hebrew), and the Brahmins (Vedic), who arbitrarily reasoned that by holding the responsibility of petitioning the god(s), they became more powerful than the god(s).

"The old regime is trying to cling to the fatalistic doctrine of divine election. The new regime recognizes the divinity of the individual; the democracy of humanity."

~ Charles Haanal

Knowledge is power and the spectrum of patriarchal philosophies presents us with countless examples of the demonization of knowledge—from the banishment of Adam and Eve from paradise for their consumption of knowledge, to the decimation of matriarchal traditions.

Ignorance begets distraction. Distraction begets ignorance.

Vanir Consciousness

"Most archeologists believed this sudden blossoming of civilization (Neolithic revolution), was driven largely by environmental changes: a gradual warming as the Ice Age ended that allowed people to begin cultivating plants and herding animals in abundance. The new research suggests this 'revolution' was actually carried out by many hands across a huge area and over thousands of years." [#094]

~ Phillip Van Doren Stern

As we quest to understand our matriarchal ancestors, I would like to point out some of the research undertaken by others. These glimpses are like pixels, and slowly, with enough glimpses, a focused picture becomes clearer.

"Homo sapiens ancestors had fully modern brains. As such, they were capable of a 'higher order consciousness' which is the ability to conceive ideas of past, present, and future, of the dreaming and waking states, and of altering consciousness. Like us, they were capable of holding on to the memories of dreams and altered consciousness experiences. As a result, this higher order consciousness allows us to remember and relate different experiences of consciousness to our every day existence. Directly because humans have this ability, ideas that are born in dreams and visionary states can be used to inform and transform everyday reality." [#104]

~ Evelyn C. Rysdyk

"Writing is the visual counterpart of speech. Marks, symbols, pictures, or letters drawn upon a surface or substrate became a graphic counterpart of the spoken word or unspoken thought.

The limitations of speech include the fallibility of human memory and an immediacy of expression that cannot transcend space and time.

The invention of writing brought people the luster of civilization and made it possible to preserve hard won knowledge, experience, and thoughts." [105]

~ Philip B. Meggs and Alston W. Purvis

Writing and symbols serve different functions. It may be understood that the value and meaning inherent within symbols is more ambiguous than the written word, in that symbols transcend subjective experience. This means the value and meaning carried by symbols can have multiple interpretations based on the experience of the individual interpreting them.

Symbols are, thus, multi-dimensional, which allows for the concealment of "levels" of value and meaning that depend upon a *specific context and experience* to be accessed and *felt*. Symbols may be understood as an ancient form of encryption technology.

The **written word** is a collection of symbols that have been formatted to contain meaning in a *generalized* way, and, thus, illusory. Words give the *impression* of implying explicit meaning, although words are interpreted and misinterpreted by the reader's *personal* experience, which makes intended meaning fallible.

Personal experience is a bias upon which we frame our picture of the world. Understanding this, oral tradition continued for centuries and still does amongst many indigenous cultures, because the written word presents knowledge in a way that can be misunderstood and misused.

"This oral tradition existed not because they had no knowledge of the art of writing but because they placed a religious prohibition on committing their knowledge to that form, in order that such knowledge should not fall into the wrong hands.

The Druids were the parallel caste to the social group, which developed in another Indo-European society—the Brahmins of the Hindu culture. There caste not only consisted of those who had a religious function but also comprised of philosophers, judges, teachers, historians, poets, musicians, physicians, astronomers, prophets, and political advisors." [#098]

~ Peter Berresford Ellis

Libido

Libido—otherwise understood as sex drive—is a biological impulse towards procreation and survival. That it *feels* pleasurable is both a blessing and a curse.

Freud focused intently on anger/violence and libido/sex because he considered these among the greatest primal drives of which most—if not all—neuroses originated.

Libido is a biological function of the body. It can operate independently of consciousness, much like the beating of your heart. Although, unlike the beating of your heart, libido can be influenced by thought. This makes libido a unique biological system that, necessarily, requires a greater *response*-ability. Because our conscious mind can influence this biological system, we become co-creators of our experience.

Our thoughts affect our ability to perform, which is the essence of the **mind-body connection**. An awareness of our biological systems on a *visceral* level allows us to adjust and modify our behaviour by synchronizing our biological instincts with desirable *qualities of behaviour* to function in support of our ideal state.

Libido is the most effective way to communicate between a biological system and consciousness. This is the essence of **Tantric** and **Taoist sexual philosophy**.

When you consider the organic engine that is our body, in which libido is the result of energy generated, we begin to understand that our ability to operate and control the movement of this energy is essential to the healthy, ongoing maintenance of the system.

A mature ego is essential to facilitating this process, by ensuring the *high chair tyrant* does not become a factor in the expression of Libido. In other words, the *qualities of behaviour* associated with the high chair tyrant (immature ego), must be absent from the sexual experience.

The high chair tyrant wants to control everything and everyone; to dominate and seek pleasure at the expense of others. These are common themes throughout pornography and the portrayal of women in society, as supported by a patriarchal worldview throughout the history of rationalism and Western thought. Regardless of daft idealism and the surface victories of feminism—which seek equality *within* the patriarchal system rather than liberation from it—society has not intrinsically changed its traditional view of women as objects of male pleasure. As long as women and men use sexuality as a currency, we will have not learned a thing.

Sexual currency reinforces desire and fear.

"The birth of Christ and the Buddha are . . . representative of the birth of our spiritual lives when we awaken to the idea that God is a projection of the energy within us, not something out there." [086]

~ Joseph Campbell

In the first centuries of Buddhism, before the Buddha was ever represented in a bodily form, he was imagined as already having left the body behind. At the foot of the world tree—the axis mundi, the "immovable spot," where one is not moved by desire and fear—he meditated. From within this silence, where mind was static and at peace, the young Buddha was visited by the *Lord of this World*—named *Kama Mara*— "desire" and "fear," which attempted to distract the Buddha from his enlightened "immovable" state. Being unable to do so, he sent his three daughters, *Desire, Fulfillment,* and *Regret*—future, present, and past—to lure him away.

Together with The Three Fates (predestination) of Greek mythology and the Three Norns (free will) of Norse mythology, we may begin to identify a pattern of elementary ideas, which form a triangle of influence that resulted from the Indo-European migration.

"The Neolithic revolution took longer to get to China and the Far East than it did to Europe. (It did not reach China until nearly 5000 years ago). But it quickly crossed the narrow straights of the Bosporus and the Dardanelles and moved into what is now Greece more than 8000 years ago." [096]

~ Philip Van Doren Stern

These Elementary Ideas gave birth to our modern conceptions of Western thought and inspired the two great world religions, Buddhism and Christianity. Incidentally, Theravada, *"word of the saints,"* Buddhism originated 500 years before the birth of Christ, and 800 years before Constantine established the official church.

Both traditions had their share of disciples who created variations on the original ideas, as evidenced by the innumerable sects that exist in either tradition today.

"Hinduism is related to Buddhism, as Judaism is to Christianity. One is born a Jew, while one professes Christianity. One is born a Hindu, while one professes Buddhism.

Buddhism and Christianity are credo religion. Credo, which means, 'I believe.' In the voluntary acceptance of Buddhism or Christianity, you are released from the biology of your birth." [086]

~ Joseph Campbell

Maintaining our ideal state is contingent upon a healthy expression of libido, and we can determine this based on the quality of our thoughts during intercourse. If you are thinking about domination, control, or violence, your movements tend to be quicker. If you are thinking about love, appreciation, and value, movement tends to be slower.

Libido is the tool by which we accelerate our internal energy-producing engine. The fuel to run this machine is the food we eat, sacrificed upon the fire of our belly.

Sex initiates a state of trance. Like any form of trance, the quality of thought while under trance has significant implications on our behaviour when not under trance. Consider the power of hypnosis as an example of the power of trance states.

By ensuring our thoughts, during sex, are of a virtuous and loving quality, sex transmutes from a single-minded source of pleasure (a weapon), into a tool, which not only maintains but also expands our ideal state.

"Altered consciousness is not only natural to our species, we have been doing it for hundreds of thousands of years. This state assists us in creating new connections between neurons. In other words, trance assists in 'rewiring' the brain. If this is true, it is not so much that shamanism is a part of our ancient way of relating to the whole world around us, it is what helped us to understand ourselves (Self-awareness), and our relationship with the world enabled us to remember the past, and ponder our future. In other words, trance contributed in creating us as a species. In addition, there are physiological and psychological benefits that occur when individuals enter trance that have been observed by scientists, not the least of which includes a better immune response."

~ Evelyn C. Rysdyk

When libido is an expression of the unity between conscious and unconscious archetypes, harmony between the Anima and Animus poles of our personal and collective psyche will be restored.

The art of Self-realization requires the maintenance of a healthy libido—an expression of love and union. The more expressions of dominance and control are required to incite our sex drive, the greater the need to transition into a period of abstinence.

Footnotes

#001 Wotan is old High German, from Wōden (Old English), from Óðinn (Old Norse).

#002 https://en.wikipedia.org/wiki/Individuation

#003 **Jordan B. Peterson**, *Personality Lecture 06*, https://www.youtube.com/watch?v=DC0faZiBcG0

#004 Jesus or the Devil. The descriptions relate to both.

#005 **Kelly McGonigal**, *The Willpower Instinct: How Self Control Works, Why It Matters, And What You Can Do to Get More of It*

#006 Schrödinger's Cat, https://www.youtube.com/watch?v=IOYyCHGWJq4

#007 www.generalsemantics.org

#008 **Charles Haanel**, *The Master Key System*

#009 Kierkegaard, Camus, Nietzsche, Heidegger, Simone de Beauvoir, etc.

#010 **Robert Moore and Douglas Gillette**, *King, Warrior, Magician, Lover: Rediscovering the Archetypes of the Mature Masculine*

#011 https://phys.org/news/2014-06-physicist-slower-thought.html

#012 **H.R. Ellis Davidson**, *Gods and Myths of Northern Europe*

#013 http://norse-mythology.org/gods-and-creatures/others/the-norns/

#014 **Marie-Louise von Franz and James Hillman**, *Lecture on Jung's typology*

#015 https://ccrma.stanford.edu/~pj97/Nietzsche.htm

#016 http://www.depthinsights.com/Depth-Insights-scholarly-ezine/e-zine-issue-3-fall-2012/jungs-reception-of-friedrich-nietzsche-a-roadmap-for-the-uninitiated-by-dr-ritske-rensma/

#017 **John Anthony West**, *Mystical Egypt* https://www.youtube.com/watch?v=rSNV5m-qOAg

#018 **Barbara Graziosi**, *The Gods of Olympus: A History* "Zeus . . . preferred the negotiations of family life to the loneliness of absolute power."

#019 **Edward F. Edinger**, *Ego and Archetype*

#020 **C.G. Jung**, *Collected Works Vol. 8*

#021 **Edred Thorsson**, *Northern Magic: Rune Mysteries and Shamanism*

#022 https://www.world-archaeology.com/features/denmark-underwater-sunken-stone-age.htm

#023 http://ngm.nationalgeographic.com/2012/12/doggerland/spinney-text

#024 https://en.wikipedia.org/wiki/Theory_of_Forms

#025 Quantum entanglement *"is a physical phenomenon that occurs when pairs or groups of particles are generated or interact in ways such that the quantum state of each particle cannot be described independently of the others, even when the particles are separated by a large distance."* i.e. time https://en.wikipedia.org/wiki/Quantum_entanglement

#026 A **swell** is a series of waves between water and air, often referred to as surface gravity waves. They are not generated by the immediate local wind, but by distant weather systems, where wind blows for the duration of time over water. This is the primary definition of a swell, as opposed to a locally generated wind wave, which is still under the influence of the mechanisms that created it, e.g. wind blowing over a puddle. More generally, a swell consists of wind-generated waves that are not—or are hardly—affected by the local wind at that time. Swell waves often have a long wavelength, but this varies due to the size, strength, and duration of the weather system responsible for the swell. The size of the water body, e.g. wavelengths, are rarely more than 150 m in the Mediterranean.

#027 http://www.globalresearch.ca/history-of-world-war-ii-nazi-germany-was-financed-by-the-federal-reserve-and-the-bank-of-england/5530318

#028 An intentional misquote by **J. C. Watts**, https://www.nytimes.com/2017/01/05/opinion/why-rural-america-voted-for-trump.html

#029 **Daniel McCoy**, *Norse Mythology For Smart People*, http://norse-mythology.org/odr-concept/

#030 https://en.wikipedia.org/wiki/Muse

#031 **Daniel McCoy**, *Norse Mythology For Smart People*, http://norse-mythology.org/gods-and-creatures/the-Æsir-gods-and-goddesses/Óðinn/

#032 **Robert Johnson**, *Inner Work*

#033 **Daniel McCoy** http://norse-mythology.org/gods-and-creatures/the-aesir-gods-and-goddesses/Friggé/

#034 http://www.bizint.com/stoa_del_sol/plenum/plenum_3.html

#035 **Edward F. Edinger**, *The Creation of Consciousness: Jung's Myth for Modern Man*

#036 https://en.wikipedia.org/wiki/Shapeshifting

#037 Durrick Walker, "Right now you are creating another illusion you just don't know what it is yet!"

#038 **Walter Copland Perry**, *The Sirens in Ancient Literature and Art*

#039 Hati and Sköll are two wolves who are chasing Sun and Moon. They are the children of Fenrir, and grandchildren of Loki. When they finally catch up with Sun and Moon, Ragnarök will be upon us.

#040 Watching the news to become aware of the suffering in the world is not compassion. This is sympathy.

#041 **Emil Carl Wilm**, *The Problem of Religion*, footnote on Pg. 114

#042 As quoted by, **H. Eves**, *Mathematical Circles Adieu*

#043 **Sir Roger Penrose**, https://www.youtube.com/watch?v=dA1_yYOoGtM

#044 **Daniel McCoy,** http://norse-mythology.org/tales/why-Óðinn-is-one-eyed/

#045 https://www.youtube.com/watch?v=mKaH-VAMGUM

#046 Dr. Bruno A. Cayoun, *Mindfulness-Integrated CBT for Well-Being and Personal Growth*

#047 In Greek mythology, Zeus—along with his brothers Poseidon and Hades—defeats the Titans, the predecessors of the Olympians. In the Roman tradition, Neptune (Poseidon) is the brother of Jupiter and Pluto.

#048 https://www.quora.com/Why-did-Tesla-say-that-3-6-9-was-the-key-to-the-universe

#049 Proto-Norse, *Wōden, Wili, Wé (Proto-Germanic *Wōdinaz, Wiljô, Wīhą)

#050 **William F. Hansen**, *Classical Mythology*

#051 https://www.ncbi.nlm.nih.gov/pubmed/10172109

#052 Composed in Iceland around the year 1220 by Icelandic historian and scholar, Snorri Sturluson.

#053 According to Plato, Atlantis was Poseidon's chosen domain.

#054 Oxford Dictionary

#055 Merriam-Webster

#056 https://www.merriam-webster.com/dictionary/psyche

#057 https://www.thevintagenews.com/2017/04/16/atacama-desert-the-driest-place-on-earth-hides-a-giant-hand-reaching-for-the-sky/

#058 **Turville-Petre**, *Myth and Religion of the North: The Religion of Ancient Scandinavia*

#059 http://norse-mythology.org/gods-and-creatures/others/Huginn-and-Muninn/

#060 **Masaru Emoto**, https://en.wikipedia.org/wiki/Masaru_Emoto

#061 A complete list can be found at https://en.wikipedia.org/wiki/List_of_names_of_Óðinn

#062 Chapter 20 of the Prose Edda book, Gylfaginning

#063 https://www.google.ca/search?q=Persona&oq=persona&aqs=chrome.0.69i59l2j69i65l2j0l2.1991j0j9&sourceid=chrome&ie=UTF-8_-q=persona+definition

#064 Yumi Sakugawa, *Your Illustrated Guide to Becoming One With The Universe*

#065 https://en.wikipedia.org/wiki/Persona

#066 http://www.dictionary.com/browse/persona

#067 **John Lindow**, *Norse Mythology: A Guide to the Gods, Heroes, Rituals, and Beliefs*

#068 **Suzannah Lipscomb**, https://www.youtube.com/watch?v=FxaVdOocgwI&t=275s

#069 https://en.wikipedia.org/wiki/Vili_and_V%C3%A9

#070 http://norse-mythology.org/concepts/Seiðr/

#071 **Dr. Yuval Noah Harari**, https://www.youtube.com/watch?v=_l3s3aRyacI&t=1178s

#072 https://www.google.ca/webhp?sourceid=chrome-instant&ion=1&espv=2&ie=UTF-8 - q=selfish

#073 https://en.wikipedia.org/wiki/Ēostre

#074 *Leap of Faith*, http://www.imdb.com/title/tt0104695/

#075 **Michio Kaku**, https://www.youtube.com/watch?v=rVWWQKU_-G0

#076 http://norse-mythology.org/gods-and-creatures/others/Mímir/

#077 https://en.wikipedia.org/wiki/Human_microbiota

#078 https://www.google.ca/webhp?sourceid=chrome-instant&ion=1&espv=2&ie=UTF-8 - q=reticular+activating+system

#079 **C.G. Jung**, *The Development of Personality*

#080 **Samael Aun Weor**, *The Perfect Matrimony*

#081 **Teresa Moorey**, *Paganism: A Beginner's Guide*

#082 https://en.wikipedia.org/wiki/Odyssey

#083 https://en.wikipedia.org/wiki/Asherah

#084 **Daniel McCoy**, For the Love of Destiny

#085 **Yngona Desmond**, *Völuspá: Seiðhr as Wyrd Consciousness*

#086 http://www.shoppbs.org/product/index.jsp?productId=13358551

#087 **C.G. Jung**, *Collected Works Vol 9*

#088 **C.G. Jung**, *The Phenomenology of the Spirit in Fairytales*

#089 https://en.wikipedia.org/wiki/Longhouse

#090 **Susan Blackmore**, Consciousness: A Very Short Introduction

#091 https://en.wikipedia.org/wiki/Occult

#092 IMDB, http://www.imdb.com/title/tt0432232/

#093 **Julian Jaynes**, The Origin of Consciousness in the Breakdown of the Bicameral Mind

#094 http://ngm.nationalgeographic.com/2011/06/gobekli-tepe/mann-text

#095 **Jean Markle**, *La Femme Celte*

#096 **Phillip Van Doren Stern**, Prehistoric Europe: From Stone Age Man to the Early Greeks

#097 **Viktor E. Frankl**, Mans Search For Meaning

#098 **Peter Berresford Ellis**, A Brief History of: The Druids

#099 Genesis 32:22-32

#100 https://en.wikipedia.org/wiki/Ask_and_Embla

#101 **Jaan Puhvel**, Comparative Mythology

#102 **Anders Hultgård**, Askr and Embla Myth in a Comparative Perspective

#103 https://journals.aps.org/pre/abstract/10.1103/PhysRevE.84.011130

#104 **Evelyn C. Rysdyk**, The Norse Shaman

#105 **Philip B. Meggs and Alston W. Purvis,** History of Graphic Design

#106 **Edward F. Edinger**, *The Creation of Consciousness: Jung's Myth for Modern Man*

Bibliography

A Brief History of: The Druids, Peter Berresford Ellis

Advanced Brain Training: Teach Yourself, Simon Wootton and Terry Horne

The Analysis of the Mind, Bertrand Russell

Askr and Embla Myth in a Comparative Perspective, Anders Hultgård

Baldr's Magic, The Power of Norse Shamanism and Ecstatic Trance, Nicholas E. Brink

Brain States, Tom Kenyon

Chaos, Gaia, Eros, Ralph Abraham

Chakras: Energy Centers of Transformation, Harish Johari

Change Your Thoughts, Change Your Life, Wayne Dyer

Civilization and its Discontents, Sigmund Freud

Comparative Mythology, Jaan Puhvel

The Complete Works of William Walker Atkinson, William Walker Atkinson

Consciousness: A Very Short Introduction, Susan Blackmore

Consciousness Became The Universe: Quantum Physics, Cosmology, Neuroscience, Parallel Universes, Roger Penrose, Stuart Hameroff, etc.

Conscious Breathing, Gay Hendricks

The Creation of Consciousness: Jung's Myth for Modern Man, Edward F. Edinger

The Culture of Make Believe, Derrick Jensen

The Diamond Approach, A.H. Almaas and John Davis

Dictionary of Northern Mythology, Rudolf Simek

The Divided Brain and The Search For Meaning, Iain McGilchrist

The Divine Science: Eternal Teachings of Authentic Mysticism, Samael Aun Weor

Dream Yoga, Samael Aun Weor

Galdrabok: An Icelandic Grimoire, Stephen E. Flowers

The Ghosts of Iceland, Robert Anderson

The Gods of Olympus: A History, Barbara Graziosi

Gods and Myths of Northern Europe, H.R. Ellis Davidson

Gurdjieff: A Beginners Guide, Gil Friedman

The Harmonies of the World, Johannes Kepler

The Head Trip: Adventures on the Wheel of Consciousness, Jeff Warren

Heidegger: Philosophy in an Hour, Paul Strathern

History of Graphic Design, Philip B. Meggs and Alston W. Purvis

I Am A Strange Loop, Douglas Hofstadter

Icelandic Magic: Practical Secrets of the Northern Grimoires, Stephen E. Flowers

Icelandic Magic: Aims, Tools, and Technique of the Icelandic Sorcerers, Christopher Alan Smith

The Indo-Europeans: In Search of a Homeland, Alain de Benoist

Inner Work: Using Dreams and Active Imagination for Personal Growth, Robert A. Johnson

The Idea of History, R.G. Collingwood

Jung: A Very Short Introduction, Anthony Stevens

A Jungian Primer: Guide to Developmental Spiritual Consciousness Theory, Thomas Pastorello

King, Warrior, Magician, Lover: Rediscovering the Archetypes of the Mature Masculine, Robert Moore and Doug Gillette

La Femme Celte, Jean Markle

Language and the Pursuit of Happiness, Chalmers Brothers

Lateral Thinking, Edward de Bono

Lectures on Jung's Typology, Marie-Louise von Franz and James Hillman

The Lonely Crowd, David Riesman

The Love of Destiny: The Sacred and Profane in Germanic Polytheism, Dan McCoy

The Magic of Maths, Arthur Benjamin

Man's Search for Meaning, Viktor E. Frankl

Maps of Meaning, Jordan Peterson

The Master Key System, Charles Haanel

Meetings with Remarkable Men, G.I. Gurdjieff

The Origin of Consciousness in the Breakdown of the Bicameral Mind, Julian Jaynes

Mind Power: The Secret of Mental Magic, William Walker Atkinson

The Modern Alchemist, Richard Miller, Iona Miller, Joel Radcliffe

My Big Toe, Thomas Campbell

Mythos, Joseph Campbell, DVD Series

The New Ambidextrous Universe: Symmetry and Asymmetry from Mirror Reflections to Superstrings, Martin Gardner

Nietzsche: Philosophy in an Hour, Paul Strathern

Nine Worlds of Seid-Magic: Ecstasy and Neo-Shamanism in North European Shamanism, Jenny Blain

The Norse Shaman, Evelyn C. Rysdyk

Northern Magic: Rune Mysteries and Shamanism, Edred Thorsson

Neuro-linguistic Programming for Dummies, Romilla Ready and Kate Burton

The Passion of the Western Mind: Understanding the Ideas That Have Shaped Our World, Richard Tarnas

Pearl of Great Price, A.H. Almaas

The Penguin Book of Norse Myths, Kevin Crossley-Holland

The Perfect Matrimony, Samael Aun Weor

Phenomenology: Basing Knowing on Appearance, Avi Sion

The Phenomenology of Spirit, Georg W.F. Hegel

Prehistoric Europe: From Stone Age Man to the Early Greeks, Phillip Van Doren Stern

A Primer of Jungian Psychology, Calvin S. Hall and Vernon J. Nordby

Psychomagic: The Transformative Power of Shamanic Psychotherapy, Alejandro Jodorowsky

Quest for the Mead of Poetry: Menstrual Symbolism in Icelandic Folk and Fairy Tales, Hallfríður J Ragnheiðardóttir

Rediscover the Magick of the Gods and Goddesses: Revealing the Mysteries of Theurgy, Jean-Louis de Biasi

Sapiens, Dr. Yuval Noah Harari

The Search for Self and the Search for God: Three Jungian Lectures and Seminars to Guide the Journey, Bud Harris

Sexuality and Anxiety: Wilhelm Reich

The Silk Roads: A New History of the World, Peter Frankopan

A Simple Guide to Being and Time, Steven Foulds

Sorcerers Screed: The Icelandic Book of Magic Spells, Skuggi

The Spiritual Journey of Alejandro Jodorowsky, Alejandro Jodorowsky

Subliminal: How Your Unconscious Mind Rules Your Behaviour, Leonard Mlodinow

The Triune Brain, Hypnosis and the Evolution of Consciousness, Adam Weishaupt

Transhumanism: A Grimoire of Alchemical Agendas, Scott de Hart and Joseph P. Farrell

The Unconscious Civilization, John Ralston Saul

The Viking Spirit: An Introduction to Norse Mythology and Religion, Daniel McCoy

Völuspá: Seiðhr as Wyrd Consciousness, Yngona Desmond

Unplugging the Patriarchy, Lucia Rene

Well-Being and Personal Growth: Four Steps to Enhance Inner Calm, Self-Confidence, and Relationships, Dr. Bruno A. Cayoun

The Willpower Instinct: How Self-Control Works, Why It Matters, and What You Can Do to Get More of It, Kelly McGonigal

The World as Will and Representation, Arthur Schopenhauer

A World Full of Gods: An Inquiry into Polytheism, John Michael Greer

Your Illustrated Guide to Becoming One With The Universe, Yumi Sakugawa

"No questions are more intricate than those which relate neither to Art alone, nor to Ethics alone, but to Art and Ethics at the same time. The philosopher, who, at the risk of displeasing everybody, embarks on such questions, must take into account both the dignity and demands of moral life, and the dignity and liberty of art and poetry."

~ Jacques Maritain

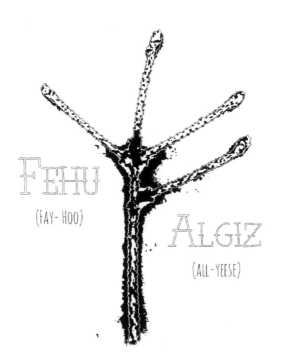

Appendix A

Excerpted from Circle Dancing, Celebrating the Sacred in Dance
© **2006 June Watts** ISBN 0 9547 2308 2
Reprinted with Permission

A Brief History of Dance

"For dancing to be a meditation—not just a social shuffle round the dance floor—it has to be total; we have to give it all we've got, getting lost in it, including out minds.

There is random, unaware movement and there is centered conscious movement. It is the latter that brings us to the state of one-pointedness, body awareness and present centeredness that is the essence of meditation."

~Louis Proto

"What I have realized after a lifetime with dance is that dance is meditation in movement, a walking into silence where every movement becomes prayer."

~Bernhard Wosein

Unlike most other species on the planet, we have always danced—fact one! Fact two—the most natural form in life is the circle. Everything natural moves in a cycle, traveling from a beginning, through middle, to an ending, which is another beginning. And yet a circle is seamless, having neither beginning nor ending.

Above us is the wheel of the heavens, the great cosmic circle dance of sun, moon, and stars. Around us is the cycle of the seasons: the springtime shoots through the summer expansion and autumn harvest, to the dying down and the returning to the earth—the composting of the old—out of which new life emerges.

The ancient people knew time was a circle not a straight line and that there were special points on the circle that called for ritual and celebration.

There are 'stations' in the cycles of the sun, the earth, and the moon; the journey of the sun across the heavens, the moon through her phases, and the seasons of the earths fertility.

The sun was honored because of its obvious and vital life sustaining warmth and light. Without it everything would die. The sun appeared constant in its cycle, but how could you be sure? It may not have been so unless rituals were religiously performed to keep it alive, to keep it turning, and call it back from the darkness each day and each year. The moon was honored because her cycles were so evident and– being changeable–she was seen as responsible for everything that moves in cycles: the fertility seasons of women and the earth. And the earth, Mother Earth, must be honored, cared for and encouraged in her cycle so that she continues to be fertile and provide food for her children, so that the Crone of the Underworld transforms into the Maiden of Spring and then into the Mother of the Harvest.

Under the wheel of the heavens and the turning of the seasons our life too is a cycle, from birth/beginning to death/ending, and on and on. Seed in the womb, seed in the earth; tender shoot, tiny babe; growing to maturity, growing to fruition; and then the release of the fruit and the return of the form and the seed to the earth, to the ground of being, to the source of life. We are a circle within a circle with no beginning and never ending.

Narrowing the lens, we have the cycle of day and night flowing ceaselessly into and out of each other. There is the breath–the energy of the life force–it too is cycles and mirrors the greater cycles with the rhythm and expansion and contraction, of rising and falling, becoming and dissolving.

Our ancestors–observing nature–saw how, for example, the movements of the moon influence many natural phenomena such as the tides, birth, the menstrual cycle. They saw their lives as cycles within cycles and echoed the circle of the earth and sun and moon in their round houses and round dances. They understood their place in the scheme of things so, naturally, they danced in a circle, and when the circle was open–as in many Greek dances–it still moved in circular form, with a leader to channel the group energy.

The famous specialist in traditional dance, Philip Thornton, who first brought Balkan dance to Britain and laid the foundation for the present repertoire of Balkan dances enjoyed in the folk dance and Sacred/Circle Dance world, describes in his book *Dead Puppets Dance* an experience he had in Albania of dance as ritual. He watched two circles, at night, dancing around a small fire of aromatic wood; twelve woman in the inner circle, twelve men in the outer. The circles were moving in opposite directions with completely different steps to the accompaniment of a drum. They were dancing the seasons, the twelve months of the year dancing around the sun/fire. When the rhythm changed and became slow and measured the men moved back and the women danced slowly bowing to the fire while the men stood still on the spot. Then with great shouts the two circles somehow became one, the rhythm sped up and the dancers danced as fast and furiously, in and out, towards and away, from the fire, gradually getting closer and closer, until–with another great shout–they all jumped into the fire and stamped it out; the sun had died and it was winter once more!

Gradually, intellect took over from the intuition, invention replaced observation, and science gave us facts. If you have a watch, you pretty soon stop relying on the position of the sun in the sky to place you in the daily cycle. Before long you don't even notice and time marches along in linear fashion, divorcing you even further from the experience of circle reality. If you are given a scientific explanation for why spring always follows winter you lose the need to invoke and work with the natural forces such as the sun and moon. If you fall sick and a quick visit to the doctor or a pill or two from the chemist give relief, you soon lose the need to observe the natural healers growing around you on the earth.

We began to hand over the sovereignty of our lives . . the line overtook the circle, time subjugated instinct and we were on the slippery slope to the disconnected, frantic, materialistic world of the 21st century–the world of quick fix–and the rush from past to future which overlooks the moment of 'now' when life happens.

This descent into dissolution of the circle has, however, been a necessary stage of our journey towards self-knowledge and awakening. The baby has no sense of its separateness, it will only gradually realize that smiles it is used to seeing up above are not a part of itself, whereas the object waving in front of its face and occasionally landing on it, is a part of itself.

We originated in a dream state, existed in tribal consciousness knowing ourselves to be part of everything. We felt each other and the plants and animals, with the same intensity as we felt ourselves. Each maiden in the ancient Beltane/May Ever sacred marriage rites in the Avebury henge in Wiltshire felt herself to be a spring flower, to be the awakened earth, and each youth a shaft of the sun. They understood– not through the intellect but instinctively–that through their coupling they were uniting earth and sun and that their dance in the ritual ecstasy was for the creation of life in the womb of the earth as well as in the human womb. But we lost this dream state of oneness with all that is; we left the Garden of Eden and began the lonely trail down into individuation. We did this in order to understand who we are. The baby slowly realizes it is a separate being and eventually understands that it can run its own life, and make choices about how to relate. We become isolated individuals so we can see the whole, each other, and ourselves, clearly and make a clear informed conscious decision to return, or not.

We are returning to the Garden but now we know; now we are aware! We have eaten of the tree of knowledge and we are able to take responsibility, knowingly, for ourselves. We re-create this truth in Sacred/Circle Dance. Sacred/Circle Dance brings individuals back into the circle consciousness. It reconnects us with a moving whole, fragments at last reunited, cells in one corporate body, the split healed.

As the line replaced the circle so the dance form changed; from something that was a community happening it progressed into straight lines, squares to couples, then to individuals dancing alone. There is no further it can go on the road to fragmentation, the limit has been reached and inevitably– although the predominant dance form is still individuals or couple–the upward curve is happening, disintegrated parts are becoming again integrated, and the circle is returning.

'We are dancing on the brink of our little world of which we know so little: we are dancing the dance of life, of death; dancing with the moon up in celebration of dimly remembered connections with out ancestors; dancing to keep the cold and darkness of a nuclear winter from chilling out bones; dancing on the brink of ecological awareness; dancing for the sake of dancing without analyzing, without rationalizing and articulating; without consciously probing for meaning but allowing meaning in being to emerge into our living space."

~Bill Devall, Deep Ecology: Living as if Nature Mattered.

Regressions

Excerpted from *Regressions: The Lengths People Will Go to Discover Authentic Love*
© 2012 Mark Allard ISBN 1-4525-5610-0
Reprinted with Permission

SERGEANT
The Killing Options.

You can feel the sun on your skin like it's burning impressions into you."

This is how he would begin writing, if we survive.

The jungle is thick, though its canopy does little to offer relief from the sun. Heat seems to rise off the ground and even the plants are prone to sweating.

The jungle is a world of its own. Smells are different. Taste is unnatural. Hearing becomes amplified, sight–diminished. Touch is a lifeline.

Creation makes a gesture of empathy towards the fools who trespass here, knowing well the inevitable destruction they must pay as the toll for entering this place.

The cost is not the same for everyone. Some pay immediately, with their life or limbs or health. Others think they got out easy, only to find themselves stalked by cyclical demons of paranoia and sabotage through countless attempts at rebuilding life away from this place.

The jungle is a jealous lover. If she can't have you, she won't let anyone.

About 100 feet from where you stand is the ocean, maybe 200 feet. It doesn't matter what direction, just pick one. **The important thing is not to doubt your Self.** Whatever pops into mind ought to be right.

The waves crash on themselves, stretching their wake onto white sands; a deceptive picture implying paradise.

That thought is not in the present. It is something you are imagining–maybe even remembering–yet somehow you know that what you are seeing in your mind's eye is *that* beach, the one two hundred feet away with crystal blue water washing up polished lava rocks on a sun soaked mirage of tranquility, until the tide once again relocates them.

The sound of a bird brings you back. Was it a bird at the beach, one from the jungle, or did it resonate from a distant memory? It is hard to tell and makes little difference. You are back. Back to the heat and the smell of your own sweat and the relief that comes with knowing the journey has to end, sometime. The tide deposited you here. The crashing waves in the distance taunt, "you can never go back," and you know it's true. You've come to far, beyond the white sand–as forbidden as a virgin–carried out by oceans breath, far beyond here, to anywhere. A great chasm separates you, and no bridge exists to take you to the other side. Within this chasm lie booby traps and landmines and snakes and killing options. There are neither trees big enough nor vines long to help you cross over. Besides, you know which direction you need to keep walking.

As if responding to the very thought in your head, the trees seem to bend at eye level, revealing a hill in the distance. It is further in front of you than the ocean is behind, and as quickly as you glimpse your destination the trees resume their original shape. There is no path for you. You must forge your own through trees that bend and sweating plants and ground that gives off heat.

It could take hours, and life–especially life in the jungle–rarely follows a straight line, but somehow you know that you will be there before the sun sets.

NOGWAL

Self-Awareness

You are in the dark.

I try hard to picture something—anything; a tree, moss, rocks, running water. You are not even able to do that. What is happening? You look around. Down at your hands and can't even see them, but you can feel them. I form a fist, and then stretch my fingers wide. If you can *feel* your hands moving but not see them, you must be blind or in the dark.

The physical you - the one with flesh and bones, is still alive. It's a place to start. **At least you aren't dead.**

The sensation of awareness travels up from your hands, through your arms and shoulders, before emptying into your chest. You become aware of your breath; the rhythmic inhale and exhale.

Now you are certain you are alive, surrounded by darkness.

Where is here? You have no memory of arriving in this dark place.

How are you feeling? *Scared. Panicked.* The words come fast and effortlessly.

What is your purpose here? *Escape.*

SERGEANT

Clean Sweep

Look down at your feet.

I am in the jungle. My boots are heavy, as if weighed down with stones. Perhaps this is just the weight of tired legs. Suddenly the boots are gone and I see golden brown feet walking effortlessly through the thick underbrush.

Boots are back on. A hill is in front of me. The destination.

I begin to see things unfold like watching a silent film; one I have already seen, which removes the suspense of it all. I am an observer, watching my alternate Self have an experience, but unable to *feel* it.

You are holding a book—a kind of encyclopedia of animals.

When I reach the snakes, I am so afraid; I can't even touch the pictures. With the tip of my finger I turn the page over. It would be better if there was something between me and the pages. You don't want to accidentally come into contact with the pictures. My touch is all that is required to awaken these frozen serpents.

I feel like I have been abandoned. The jungle is hot and my clothes are sticky. Why are you here alone? What happened to everyone? I can't remember, but I feel like we have been misjudged.

I see something red in the trees. Maybe a bird. I keep walking.

Family vacation. You are six or seven? I am sitting in the sand with some toys. As the water rolls in a snake emerges and slithers towards me. You are frozen. Will it end like this? I know what snakes can do.

A few feet in front of me it rears up, standing within its scaled cocoon. Its tongue hisses at me. Our eyes meet.

Memories . . . like shards of ice on a still pond that have shattered. The broken pieces have begun to drift away. I must bring them back. I must do this before it's too late. If I could collect the pieces, I could reform a surface that would allow me to see my own reflection. For now, all I see are fragments.

Red in the trees. Boots on. Boots off. What am I missing?

It feels like I have been left here. *Abandonment.*

I hear a voice sing to me - the memory of some child's lullaby I have forgotten.

What am I running from? Who have I abandoned? Who or what am I running *to*?

I escape the beach. I am crying and screaming because I am so afraid. My body is vibrating. I run to where my parents and their friends are, but no one will believe me. As if I even want their attention. I wouldn't have mentioned it but you are afraid, and fear makes people do unstable things.

You don't believe me! I saw a snake. Why does no one ever believe me? Why do they always think I am lying? Can't they see what they are doing to me? I will grow up and doubt myself, sheltering what I really think and feel because if I express myself, people will misinterpret me. They will think I am lying. Why can't they see this?

It came out of the water and headed straight for me. It stood in its scaled cocoon and our eyes met. I don't know why it stopped. I don't know why it let me live. Maybe because not being believed is worse.

I am not a liar. Why won't they believe me? Is this how it will end?

When I was ten years old there was a stairway in my closet, leading up to the attic. What existed beyond that door filled me with as much excitement as it did trepidation. It wasn't just an attic, it was a way out. It was change.

What if that world turns out to be more horrible than the one I already know? I don't want to be stuck there. What if opening that door means things will never be the same?

I would hate to discover cobwebs and mothballs. I think that would be a worse fate than never opening it at all. **Sometimes the hope of a thing is better than an absolute.**

You think about this entirely too much. My logic begins to question if the door is not there to be opened, but guarded. Perhaps it is your responsibility to make sure the door stays closed. Maybe this is why I was put here, at this specific time in history.

I think I am going to wait. In an emergency, it won't matter if it is the right thing to do or not. It won't matter if I find cobwebs and mothballs. The only thing that will matter is that I have an escape.

I have no memories of ever opening the attic door, though I find it hard to accept I never tried. Two years we lived in that house. Perhaps those memories were wiped away.

I believe in that kind of thing. I believe our higher Self works with the body to create the circumstances we call life. It does this because there is a point to us being here. *Something we have forgotten.* **The events of life are just exercises in remembering.** The catch is, what doesn't make you stronger kills you.

It's a temporary solution, losing memories. It does some good in the short term, but **no one can outrun the toll, not even by denying the consequences of choices or downplaying their relevance.** Our choices determine whom we become.

Memories are a lot like dreams. The ones I forget are—without a doubt—the most significant.

I must be getting close now. The sun is about to set and I know I will arrive before then. The jungle is so thick it is hard to tell how close I am or how far I've come.

NOGWAL

Mistaken For Dead

A terrifying thought occurs to me. What if I am in a wooden box, deep in the ground? I once read about a casket that was designed with a kind of pipe leading to the surface to provide air for someone in this very situation.

I suppose you would have a few days of screaming before your body resigned itself to die; hopefully before your stomach began eating itself.

I believe that kind of thing happens—that we can make a decision and just say, "I'm done," and the darkness closes in. **A kind of joyful resignation, like suicide without ever pulling the trigger.**

The longer you lie here, the harder it becomes to have any hope that I will be saved.

I can only imagine the oxygen casket was designed because someone was buried alive and survived the ordeal. What a thought. Imagine being that guy?

Something must have been terribly wrong with his body to go into shut down mode—enough that he was mistaken for dead. Then to wake up, find yourself in the dark, come to the conclusion that you are buried and dig yourself out—that's got to change you. It would change everything. Every perspective would be re-evaluated. Every belief system would be challenged.

Whoever that guy was—who inspired the ultimate insurance policy against premature burial—they must have worshipped him.

How could you resolve that I was not legitimately dead? That no mistake had been made? Rather some greater force had chosen to resurrect us for some great purpose?

The sheer panic of waking up in darkness and clawing my way to emancipated freedom–fingers bleeding and caked with blood and splinters–this has got to be significant.

Why are we required to dig himself out of the ground? Is it essential to the process of resurrection; a mandatory requirement?

What strange and sympathetic magic orchestrates this kind of event?

It's not everyone who comes back from the dead. By the time they figured it out–if they did–that he was just like the rest of them, the truth would have been irrelevant. He was a God of the New World.

The One They Call the Vision

A Place I Visit With My Eyes Closed

It is the sensation of moving very quickly. I am flying above fields towards the Glenn.

I descend through a canopy of trees that shield the magic contained within this ancient place. The faerie forest, she calls it.

Something is different this time. The colors are more vibrant. This place is more alive and more intimidating in its stillness.

It is snowing lightly. All of the green is peppered with glistening white.

I picture myself here with her in a different time. I am standing in the trunk of a tree that is split down the center, forming a kind of archway. She calls this the doorway for faeries to enter our world.

These memories are like dreams to me. A place I visit with my eyes closed.

As the branches part, I see a body lying in the snow. His arms are spread open like the ascending Christ. His blackened hair with red hues is wet and the melting snow gives it shine. Furs are wrapped around his body. A blanket of crimson soaks the snow beneath him.

I come to realize that the body lying in the snow is me. I can't explain how I am watching myself or floating through the air and descending through the trees. I don't know where I am coming from or where I am headed. These memories belong to me. I am *that* body and *this* essence.

It has been such a long journey. I have been away for so long.

Your eyes flutter in the falling snow. My body is cold but there are warm spots. Why are you lying here? Why did I come here?

As quickly as you ask, I find myself transported.

SERGEANT

The Switch

Imagination is a word grownups use to imply pretending, but only because they have forgotten what it's like. I don't pretend. I create worlds.

I often wonder if that is why I got electrocuted. Did I mention that? It happened when I was eleven. My body was bouncing off the floor. It was that bad. I could have died. Instead, I lost my childhood. It seems entirely possible that I was electrocuted because I saw too much. Things I needed to see and then forget until the time was right to remember. I believe that time is now.

Sometimes I think parents have this idea that imagination works like a switch, as though it can be turned on and off—convenient when you send your children away to play, inconvenient when you are trying to sleep and they are screaming about people in their room with machine guns and snakes all over the floor.

Before I was electrocuted, I saw a lot of things differently— people and animals and sickness. I could see a headache and pull it out like a string.

Something is travelling above me. I can hear it. I look up but can't tell what it is through the thickness of the trees. Occasionally its shadow descends— then disappears—and it is moving too fast for me to make out its shape. It makes a sound like the banging of a drum, and another . . . a humming. To be honest, I find it comforting. I don't feel so lonely.

In *Living Mythos*, filmmaker and musician Mark Allard ventures into the heart of the metaphor contained within his first book, *Regressions* (2012), and begins to expose the mechanics at the heart of the multiverse that is the human psyche.

Continuing the adventure: Internal dialogues are projected as a cast of mysterious beings, who come to life over a game of HNEFATAFL. Watch this short film at www.visceralmfi.com

Visit us online at:

http://www.visceralmfi.com

https://www.instagram.com/visceralmfi/

https://www.facebook.com/visceralmfi/

https://twitter.com/visceralmfi

Made in the USA
San Bernardino, CA
14 February 2018